The Education Adviser
Raising the quality of education
advice and support

Advising on
School
Improvement

ASSOCIATION
of EDUCATION
ADVISERS

CRITICAL
PUBLISHING

THE EDUCATION ADVISER SERIES

Take a look at all the titles in this series.

- *The Role of the Education Adviser*
- *Advising on School Improvement*
- *Advising on Governance in Education*
- *Advising on Organisational Development in Education*
- *Advising on Change Management in Education*
- *Advising on Implementing Quality Systems in Education*

Acknowledgements

The development of the AoEA book series has been an important milestone for the Association and this second book focuses on school improvement. The range of chapters capture the innovative work of our Associates and friends of our organisation but they also crystallise the journey of the AoEA which has included the construction of criteria, establishing processes of accreditation and widespread professional learning and conversation. This book, from a wide range of perspectives, captures the energy, debates and approaches at the heart of school improvement advisory work.

With this in mind, I'd like to extend my thanks to the editorial team, to each of our authors and to the publishing team who, in a very short period of time, have contributed to bringing this book to publication. A huge amount of energy, reflection and craft has gone into creating such an engaging and varied text, which is hugely appreciated.

Les Walton, CBE
Executive Chair of the AoEA

To order, or for details of our bulk discounts, please go to our website www.criticalpublishing.com or contact our distributor, Ingram Publisher Services (IPS UK), 10 Thornbury Road, Plymouth PL6 7PP, telephone 01752 202301 or email IPSUK.orders@ingramcontent.com. Details of bulk order discounts can be found at www.criticalpublishing.com/delivery-information.

Our titles are also available in electronic format: for individual use via our website, and for libraries and other institutions from all major ebook platforms.

First published in 2024 by Critical Publishing Ltd

British Library Cataloguing in Publication Data
A CIP record for this book is available from the British Library

ISBN: 978-1-916925-40-3

This book is also available in the following e-book formats:
EPUB ISBN: 978-1-916925-41-0
Adobe e-book ISBN: 978-1-916925-42-7

Text and cover design by Out of House Limited
Project Management by Newgen Publishing UK

Critical Publishing
3 Connaught Road
St Albans
AL3 5RX

www.criticalpublishing.com

Contents

About the AoEA and the editorial team

About the AoEA

The vision of the AoEA is that every school, college and education provider has access to high-quality support, advice and challenge, which is independent and focused on improving outcomes for children, schools and their communities.

The AoEA's mission is to provide an accredited quality standard, to offer continuous professional learning aligned to the standard and to create an international community for those who support schools, colleges, and other education providers.

About the editorial team

Dr Tony Birch, Series Editor

Tony is author of *Understanding Primary Education as a Whole* and Founding Director of Birch Education, an educational consultancy dedicated to empowering individuals and teams to develop high quality, sustainable approaches. Previously Tony worked for Bolton Council for more than 20 years: as a school improvement adviser and head of school improvement before becoming the lead for education and learning strategy.

Ian Lane, Chair of the Editorial Team

Following headship of an inner-city secondary school, Ian joined a local authority advisory service as a senior adviser and was later appointed Director of School Improvement for the same 'core city'. In more recent years, he has held CEO roles in both a primary and a secondary school's multi-academy trust and worked as an independent school improvement adviser.

Les Walton, CBE, Executive Chair of the AoEA

Les' career spans pivotal changes in education since the 1960s. His book, *Education the Rock and Roll Years*, is described by Professor Andy Hargreaves as 'visionary ... An excellent piece of writing'. Les has been a headteacher, director of education and founder and principal of a further education college. He has also had significant, regional and national influence. He founded Northern Education Associates and Schools North-East. Nationally, he chaired the Young People's Learning Agency and assisted its transition to the Education and Skills Funding Agency. He has also been a key adviser to multiple UK Secretaries of State. Les received the OBE in 1996 and CBE in 2013 for his services to education.

Eric Halton, Non-Executive Director of the AoEA

Over a period of 13 years, Eric's leadership in primary headships significantly improved inclusive provision, high-quality outcomes for children, resulting in outstanding inspection ratings. During this time, he also held a number of school-to-school system roles as consultant to individual schools, building professional practice networks. Eric, in more recent years, was head of a highly regarded school inspection and advisory service, which spanned more than one local authority.

Mary Lowery, Head of School Improvement, Northern Ireland

Mary has over 20 years' teaching experience in two urban integrated comprehensive colleges in Derry and Belfast and has been part of the development of integrated education in Northern Ireland since its early days. Mary joined the Education and Training Inspectorate (ETI) in 2014, inspecting across educational phases and supporting the development of models of inspection and self-evaluation, before moving into school development work with the Education Authority in 2018. In 2019, she co-founded WomenEdNI, which connects and inspires women in educational leadership.

Mairéad Mhig Uaid, Head of School and System Improvement, Northern Ireland

Mairéad has 20 years' experience in school senior leadership, bringing about both school and system-wide improvement. Her experience extends beyond organisational settings to design and delivery of tailored curriculum, resource and Teacher Professional Learning. Mairéad leads school and system improvement through a people-centric coaching style.

Peter Parish, AoEA Development Team

Peter formerly led a School Improvement Service in a local authority in the North-East of England. During this time the Council was awarded Beacon Council status for 'Tackling School Failure'. He also co-ordinated successful funding proposals for major education projects. He then became Head of Planning, Commissioning and Quality Assurance in the council's Children's Services. In 2010 he became Director of Operations for a large multi-academy trust.

Lauren Hanson, AoEA Central Team

Lauren is currently completing a graduate internship programme set up by Sunderland University, and has been with the AoEA since September 2022. Lauren runs the AoEA Professional Learning Programme for education advisers, which provides both online and face to face seminars as well as fortnightly Education Keeping In Touch (EduKIT) meetings throughout the academic year. She works alongside members of the AoEA Development Team, as well as several external experts, to ensure that the programme runs smoothly.

About the contributors

Stuart Adlam, Associate School Improvement Manager, Hampshire County Council

Stuart has been the headteacher of three primary schools and has held senior leadership roles in primary and all-through schools both in the UK and overseas. He has experience as a primary phase inspector/adviser and currently works with the primary strategy team for Hampshire County Council. Stuart has a particular interest in professional learning for new and established headteachers; he designs and delivers leadership programmes for senior leaders in Hampshire and beyond.

Professor Mel Ainscow CBE, Emeritus Professor, University of Manchester

Mel is also Professor of Education at the University of Glasgow and Adjunct Professor at Queensland University of Technology. A long-term consultant to UNESCO, Mel is internationally recognised as an authority on the promotion of inclusion and equity in education. Examples of his writing can be found in *Struggles for Equity in Education: The Selected Works of Mel Ainscow* (Routledge World Library of Educationalists series). In the Queen's 2012 New Year Honours list, Mel was made a CBE for services to education.

Michaela Barber, Primary Phase Inspector, Hampshire County Council

Michaela is an advocate for continuous professional development and is driven to ensure high quality training for the development of teachers and leaders at all levels. Following various leadership roles, including headships in both the UK and internationally, Michaela is a primary phase Inspector and educational adviser for Hampshire County Council. As part of the role, Michaela has been instrumental in supporting Hampshire's early career teachers and those new to the teaching profession.

Dr Kate Chhatwal, OBE, CEO of Challenge Partners

Dr Kate Chhatwal is CEO of the national school improvement charity Challenge Partners. A former senior civil servant and teaching school executive director, Kate is Non-Executive Director of Olex.AI; Independent Chair of Liverpool Priority Area and Chair of ImpactEd's Education Advisory Board. She also served as a trustee for eight years for STEP Academy Trust. In 2015, Kate co-founded the Leading Women's Alliance to tackle the under-representation of women in senior education roles. Kate holds a PhD in education policy and has been awarded an OBE for her services to education.

Clare Evans, Principal of St Teresa's Nursery School, West Belfast, Northern Ireland

Clare is a dedicated and accomplished educator with nearly three decades of experience as an advisory teacher, regional capacity building officer, and principal of a nursery school in West Belfast. Clare is an active member of her Area Learning Community and has demonstrated her commitment to leading and managing a school that meets every child at their point of need. Her holistic approach places both children and stakeholders at the heart of her efforts to drive school and system improvement.

Narinder Gill, School Improvement Director, Elevate Multi-Academy Trust

Narinder is School Improvement Director for Elevate Multi-Academy Trust, a primary Trust in North Yorkshire. She has worked in education for more than 30 years, successfully leading three schools as a headteacher. Her last school was the subject of her recent publication *Creating Change in Urban Settings,* which charts the journey and impact of curriculum and leadership development during challenging times. Narinder is a strategic director for the Curriculum Foundation and has been working on the development of the curriculum in South Sudan. As an accredited executive business coach, Narinder has worked with schools, trusts, the NHS and the private sector.

Tom Grieveson, AoEA Development Team

Tom has extensive experience of school and system-wide improvement and inspection. He worked as a senior HMI (Her Majesty's Inspector) with Ofsted within the North-East Yorkshire and Humberside senior leadership team. He has consistently led some of the most high-profile section 5 and section 8 inspections in several parts of England. Prior to joining HMI, Tom was a headteacher in two schools covering a 12-year period and held senior positions in local authority school improvement teams, including as Head of Service.

Professor David Hopkins

Professor David Hopkins has been chief adviser to three Secretaries of State on School Standards in the United Kingdom, Dean of Education at the University of Nottingham, consultant to the Organisation for Economic Co-operation and Development (OECD) and World Health Organization (WHO), adviser to some 20 Ministries globally and a secondary school teacher, as well as an international mountain guide. He was recently ranked as the 16th most influential educator in the world. His latest book, *Unleashing Greatness*, was published in June 2024.

Rebecca Jackson, Headteacher, Cragside Primary School

Rebecca is the headteacher of a highly successful, large primary school in Newcastle-upon-Tyne, in the North East of England. Her career spans more than 30 years, during which time she has worked as a learning support assistant, a classroom teacher and an EOTAS (education other than at school) tutor. She has been a headteacher for ten years.

Kevan Naughton, Headteacher, The Valley Community School

Kevan has, for more than 20 years, successfully led his schools through numerous Ofsted inspections maintaining outstanding outcomes. His urban school, situated in an area of high socio-economic disadvantage, regularly performs in the top 500 schools nationally. Kevan is a national leader in education and has supported many schools to improve. He was a key part of the early DFE trials into mentoring and coaching for early career teachers. In recent years Kevan has worked as an Ofsted inspector and inspects maintained, academy and independent schools.

Emma Tarrant, Inspector/Adviser for English, Hampshire County Council

Emma is a specialist English inspector/adviser for Hampshire County Council, overseeing a subject advisory team as well as contributing to county strategy. She has extensive experience of working with senior and middle leaders: advising schools and MATs across Hampshire, Oxfordshire, Bournemouth and Poole.

Chris Zarraga, Director of Schools North East

Chris has been part of the Schools North East team since its inception in 2007. In 2007, he was appointed Director. Chris works with school leaders across the North East to represent the voice of all 1,150 schools from across the region. Together, they strive to influence national education policy and ensure that the North East is at the forefront of educational debate. Chris also works nationally with the wider education and charity sectors.

Introduction to the AoEA and the purpose of the book series

LES WALTON, CBE

The purpose of this book is to support the professional learning of those who are involved in education and providing support to others, including those currently engaged as leaders in educational settings and those who are advising and supporting them.

As we move deeper into the third decade of the twenty-first century, the need to redesign the process by which schools are supported and enabled to improve has become increasingly important. In 2016, a meeting was held in the Department for Education headquarters in London. Key national school and college representative organisations were present, and all agreed that there was a need to quality assure and develop the quality of advice and support received by schools.

Following an intensive research and development programme, it was decided to establish the Association of Education Advisers (AoEA), which is independent of national and local government. It was also decided that the AoEA should provide an accredited international standard that would be relevant to all schools, colleges and education providers across the United Kingdom, and ultimately throughout the world.

The AoEA has a vision that every school and college, no matter its size or designation, has access to high-quality support, advice and challenge, which is independent and focused on improving outcomes for children and young people, their schools, their colleges and their communities.

There are 36,000 schools across the United Kingdom alone. The core message from those who support and advise on school improvement to those who lead and inspect is that we should 'professionalise' the role of the adviser. A major part of the work of the AoEA has been in developing the professional community within the United Kingdom and internationally for those who support and advise schools, colleges and other education providers.

This accredited national and international community of advisers is increasing daily. We believe that we are at the very beginning of our journey and that, at the outset, we seriously underestimated the potential of an international community of education advisers. We don't anymore!

We believe that those who lead, inspect and advise schools should have access to accredited standards and continuous professional learning. The three points of this triangular relationship are all necessary. If one part is weakened, then the whole system becomes unsustainable.

Advising and supporting colleagues within schools and colleges over which you may not have direct power and control requires a unique set of skills and knowledge. The hundreds of educationalists who have achieved the AoEA accredited standard tell us they value most highly the independent nature of the AoEA, the opportunity to reflect on their work through a rigorous accreditation process and associated professional learning. They tell us that the AoEA process provides:

- an opportunity to reflect on their own practice through external eyes, and to condense and showcase their contribution to organisational improvement;
- a valuable opportunity to receive external affirmation and feedback, while also having signposted opportunities for further learning.

It helps them to:

- validate their ability to advise others;
- understand their own skills and expertise in relation to how they can support others;
- develop further and hone their skills and expertise in supporting others;
- make others aware of their knowledge, skills and experience, thereby strengthening the educational advisory network and the potential for increased learning and support from one another.

In harnessing the strengths of our growing membership, this series of books, entitled 'The Education Adviser', will provide some of the most up-to-date thinking and examples of good practice from across the

United Kingdom and internationally. If you provide advice and support or lead a school and college, then the aim of this series of books is to provide some essential reading. The AoEA has selected contributors from the 400 plus accredited AoEA Associates and partners together with well-known experts from across the United Kingdom and beyond.

All contributors have mastery in their specific area, whether that is how to demonstrate professional credibility, understanding what causes a school's success or failure, developing a school improvement strategy, supporting major change programmes or using quality-improvement tools such as Kaizen.

The books in this series are:

1. *The Role of the Education Adviser*

2. *Advising on School Improvement*

3. *Advising on Governance in Education*

4. *Advising on Organisational Development in Education*

5. *Advising on Change Management in Education*

6. *Advising on Implementing Quality Systems in Education*

This book, *Advising on School Improvement,* is the second in our series. We hope you will enjoy reading it and that it will contribute to your professional learning and work as an education adviser wherever you may be working in supporting and in advising school and college leaders.

Introduction to Book 2: *Advising on School Improvement* – a repertoire of skills and approaches

DR TONY BIRCH

In this second book in the series, the focus moves from advisory skills to school improvement. The focus on the repertoire of advisory skills in Book 1 illustrated how advisers, to use Kevin McDermid's typology, use a not inconsiderable repertoire of mentoring, performance management, coaching, training, ongoing advice, constructive criticism, motivating and persuading as vehicles for the Association of Education Advisers' (AoEA) criteria: strong personal attributes and skills; offering considered challenge; enabling others through support and expertise; enabling transference of knowledge; and doing this through the credibility and earned authority developed in their field. The movement here is to focus more specifically on the adviser's expertise in school improvement: the multidimensional and continuous developments that shape processes of teaching and learning.

'School improvement' is, of course, an expansive field full of complexity. A brief scan of the scope of, for example, Brighouse and Waters (2021) reveals high-level themes that include curriculum, pedagogy, assessment, leadership, school climate, admissions, attendance, exclusions, behaviour, SEND, parents, community, governance, accountability and finance. Moreover, as Professor David Hopkins (2022) illustrates, the emphasis of school improvement has evolved over time from a focus on the adoption of curriculum materials in the 1960s, through understanding processes of implementation in the 1970s, to the 'school effectiveness' and 'school improvement' movements, and subsequent approaches to large-scale system reform. Debates continue about which policy levers and strategies have most value.

In addition, educational settings and the systems in which they are nested have many components, which interact with one another. Contexts vary and every setting has its own trajectory: people, policies, processes, pedagogies and performance differ. If, at a theoretical level, advising on school improvement may appear simple, in practice it has high levels of contextual nuance. School improvement's importance may be axiomatic but the adviser's role is vital in skilfully supporting the identification of need, pinpointing priorities, helping to build capacity and making 'development work' meaningful while capturing the spirit, based on Dylan Wiliam's (2012) suggestion that we seek to improve our schools not because they are not good enough but because they can be even better.

Described in these terms, advising for school improvement is highly skilled work: a combination that demands from school improvement advisers (SIAs) an understanding of how schools and the education system work, high levels of expertise in their field and the ability to translate knowledge into continuous improvement. In this vein, the AoEA's criteria are illustrative. Advising on school improvement demands:

- working in concert with the school's leadership;

- providing clear, insightful and well-written reports;

- understanding causal factors impacting on performance;

- critically evaluating a range of domains (performance, leadership, pedagogy, governance);

- having up-to-date knowledge of relevant educational policy, inspection and other related issues.

In this spirit Andy Hargreaves (2024), referring to earlier work on sustainable leadership, argues – and we can apply this to the successful and effective SIA's work: It focuses on things that matter. It persists over time. It requires collective responsibility. It must not have a negative impact on other schools and communities in the surrounding environment. It prospers from diverse environments and leadership teams. It renews rather than depletes people's energy. And it conserves the best of the past in moving forward to a stronger future.

The three Cs of the school improvement adviser

The role of the SIA has many dimensions, and the field is diverse and complex, but in this book we have grouped the contributions under three themes: context and causality; capacity-building; and collaboration.

Understanding the dimensions of context and causality in educational settings is a key skill of the SIA as they explore the contexts in which they are engaged, and this is the focus of Part 1. What is unique about this situation? Are practices effective? Why have they been chosen? Who and what has influenced and shaped them? Are there lessons to be learned from research or evidence? A key role of the SIA is to delve into 'root causes', bringing knowledge, expertise and evidence to the situation to pinpoint priorities for action.

Part 2 focuses on 'capacity-building': put simply this *refers to any effort being made to improve the abilities, skills, and expertise of educators'* (EdGlossary, 2024). This is the process of developing, strengthening and sustaining the knowledge and skills at play in the setting and understanding whether they are sufficient to realise change. If not, the challenge is identifying and sourcing the 'active ingredients' (Educational Endowment Fund, 2024) that are needed. This is a key role for the SIA as they support the creation of self-sustaining settings and systems.

'Collaboration' is the focus of Part 3, which explores the process of enabling people and settings to work together with others to create collective impact. The school improvement adviser has a key role in creating connections and supporting the transfer of expertise.

Part 1: Understanding context and causality

Dylan Wiliam (2018) comments that everything works somewhere, nothing works everywhere and the first two chapters in Part 1 help us to explore this from the SIA's perspective. They describe why understanding context and causality are critical to securing timely, effective and ultimately meaningful school improvement advice.

Chapter 1 by Les Walton provides insight into the wider context and why it matters so much for advisers to understand this fully in order to advise effectively. Education advisers, he argues, need to work with leaders in helping them to understand the wider landscape and the key external drivers for change, which impact on sustainable school improvement. He argues that building strong, trusting relationships, both within a school or setting and externally, will enable a shared understanding of the challenges facing the school and its community.

In Chapter 2, Tom Grieveson takes this to the school level and focuses on understanding, identifying and addressing the causal factors that impact on a school's improvement, building firmly on the foundation laid in Chapter 1.

Three chapters then follow that help to exemplify these aspects. First, in Chapter 3, Rebecca Jackson describes how, as an adviser, she was able to explore the causal and contextual factors that existed in an already successful school. She describes the process of critically analysing the context of the school and working with the staff and community to ensure greater equity in the school's offering. She describes it as a *'tale of marginal gains and slow improvements rather than quick wins and rapid change'.*

In Chapter 4, Stuart Adlam describes how important the needs of new headteachers are, and how their priorities vary according to their experience, context and the needs of their schools. The way advice is constructed should be context sensitive, and it can be a vital factor in their success. Stuart also comments that the approach should be longitudinal:

> *We should be viewing headteacher induction as the start of a process of support and development that continues deep into headship. We should be aiming to continue to provide high quality professional learning.*

Mairéad Mhig Uaid writes reflectively about her own experience with Irish Medium Education (IME) in Chapter 5. With humility, she explains how her work both shaped and was shaped by this involvement. This development is particularly context specific as she describes the growth of IME over time, the practices that were developed and the sustained commitment that has led to the current position of IME.

Finally in this section, in Chapter 6 Kevan Naughton demonstrates how an understanding of the global context guided his own thinking. He considers the emphasis placed on curriculum reform within the Global Educational Reform Movement. He considers a profile of systemic 'pillars' that are needed to support and underpin curriculum development and teaching. From his personal knowledge and understanding of what it means to be evidence informed, he explains how through his analyses he was able to develop the factors into a working model that would lead from successful approaches to implementation.

Part 2: Building capacity in school improvement

An understanding of causal and contextual factors should lead to developmental activity and mean that subsequent improvement processes are then brought to bear. Part 2 focuses on capacity-building as a vital component of the SIA's approach.

Professor David Hopkins begins this section in Chapter 7 with an expansive exploration of the field of school improvement and its implications for advisers. From his experience of leading major national and international projects, he argues that research evidence suggests advisory support is far more effective when a proven strategy is utilised to focus developmental activity and channel energy. 'Unleashing greatness' offers the key components of such a 'capacity-building' strategy. David argues that a compelling and well-articulated moral purpose can provide inspiration and is then supported through clarity of focus at the classroom level and a way of working that enables leaders and teachers to learn from one another. Leaders' and teachers' energies, he argues, should be focused on where impact will be greatest for all groups of learners: in improving the quality of classroom practice.

Four chapters then follow that illustrate capacity-building in practice. Each is different in approach: the contexts are clearly different, but the developments are inherently powerful in building skills, expertise and confidence.

A systematic approach is not to be underestimated and Chapter 8 by Emma Tarrant, which focuses on supporting middle leaders, suggests just this. She describes several challenges commonly faced by middle leaders, including role ambiguity, workload pressures and a lack of appropriate experience. She explains how they benefit from ongoing support and professional development to enhance their leadership skills and effectiveness in driving school improvement.

Michaela Barber, meanwhile, turns to the challenge of supporting new teachers. She argues in Chapter 9 that advisers can play an important role in ensuring schools have the capacity to support the recruitment and retention of early career teachers (ECTs), in part by evaluating the extent to which a school is making effective provision for ECTs' development and helping to address any emerging performance issues. She also describes how supporting an effective Learning Community for ECTs in the wider educational community builds professional resilience.

In a similar vein, but in a contrasting context – from the perspective of a multi-academy trust – in Chapter 10 Narinder Gill shows how, through a process of continual improvement, expertise can be developed within an organisation and contribute to its growing capacity.

In Chapter 11, Ian Lane explores the school-specific work needed to realise the kind of change advocated by David Hopkins. In this case, he reports how important it is for headteachers to be 'seen and heard', but also subtly and skilfully challenged in making improvements that fit contextually; in this way, improvement is both enabled and secured.

Finally, to bring this section to a close, in Chapter 12, Peter Parish explains a vital component of capacity-building: the school improvement plan. Peter's chapter is a reminder that by careful analysis, through precision-driven priorities and involving the whole team, more time and energy can be expended more effectively and the change processes deepened.

Part 3: Supporting collaborative school improvement

Part 3 opens with Chapter 13 by Professor Mel Ainscow. He illustrates, from two major regional and national projects, how working together is more effective than working alone. Mel reflects on his work within two government-instigated improvement initiatives: the Greater Manchester Challenge from 2007 to 2011, and Schools Challenge Cymru from 2014 to 2017. Both projects involved teams of what were called 'challenge advisers' and focused on finding ways to break the link between disadvantaged home backgrounds and educational outcomes (Ainscow, Chapman and Hadfield, 2020). He argues that:

> *While increased collaboration of the sort mentioned in this chapter is vital as a strategy for promoting equity, the experience of the two Challenge projects shows that it is not enough. The essential additional ingredient is an engagement with evidence that can bring an element of mutual challenge to such collaborative processes.*

Three examples of partnership working follow.

Dr Kate Chhatwal's account of the Challenge Partners model in Chapter 14 offers an example of systemic collaboration in action. She describes how Challenge Partners operates as a national practitioner-led education charity accelerating school improvement, leadership development and pupil progress, and how it shares practice across schools and trusts through rigorous peer reviews, tailored school improvement programmes and national and local collaboration. Kate concludes:

> *The important job of school improvement needn't be a solo endeavour ... collaboration should be hard-edged, demanding high standards of rigour and evidence to inform evaluation and action, harnessing and amplifying the ordinary magic of practitioner insight and dialogue.*

Schools North East is a partnership across a region. In Chapter 15, Chris Zarraga explains how Schools North East acts as a representative voice for all headteachers from across the region in helping regional challenges to be better understood by policy-makers and educationalists nationally. Chris explains that to be truly collaborative and representative of the region's needs, all the organisation's activity has to be focused on the schools' identified priorities, school-led and/ or co-constructed with school leaders.

Finally, in Northern Ireland, Clare Evans describes the process of creating and leading effective collaboration across the nursery sector in Chapter 16. Her collaborative group established dissolvable clusters and resource hubs to foster effective knowledge-sharing. Through collaborative training and support, they empower schools to address children's emotional and developmental needs, based on six nurture principles and trauma-informed practice.

The chapters in this book bring together the themes of context and causation, capacity-building and collaboration. Collectively, they help to illustrate the repertoire of knowledge, skills and understandings deployed by the SIA in a range of situations and settings.

References

Ainscow, M, Chapman, C and Hadfield, M (2020) *Changing Education Systems: A Research-based Approach*. London: Routledge.

Brighouse, T and Waters, M (2021) *About Our Schools: Improving on Previous Best*. Camarthen: Crown House.

EdGlossary (2024) *The Glossary of Educational Reform*. [online] Available at: www.edglossary.org/capacity (accessed 7 May 2024).

Education Endowment Fund (2024) *Putting Evidence to Work: A School's Guide to Implementation*. [online] Available at: https://d2tic4w voliusb.cloudfront.net/eef-guidance-reports/implementation/EEF-Act ive-Ingredients-Summary.pdf?v=1635355218 (accessed 3 June 2024).

Hargreaves, A (2024) *Leadership from the Middle: The Beating Heart of Educational Transformation*. London: Routledge.

Hopkins, D (2022) The Role of Networks in Supporting School Improvement. In Handscomb, G and Brown, C (eds) *The Power of Professional Learning Networks* (pp 27–42). Woodbridge: John Catt Educational.

Wiliam, D (2012) How Do We Prepare Our Students for a World We Cannot Possibly Imagine? Keynote speech at SSAT National Conference, AAC Liverpool, 4–5 December.

Wiliam, D (2018) *Creating the Schools Our Children Need: Why What We're Doing Now Won't Help Much, and What We Can Do Instead.* West Palm Beach, FL: Learning Sciences International.

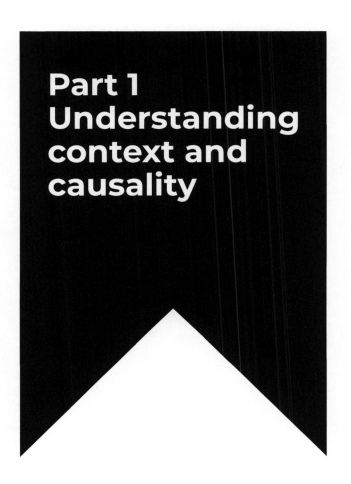

Part 1
Understanding context and causality

1 Understanding school improvement within a wider context

LES WALTON, CBE

Key learning

- Schools don't exist in isolation. They are an integral part of a wider community and society, wherever in the world they are located.

- Education advisers working with school leaders need to understand this wider context and the key external drivers for change, which impact on sustainable school improvement.

- Building strong, trusting relationships, both within the school and externally, will assist in enabling a shared understanding of the challenges facing the school and its community.

- This, in turn, will lay the foundation for a collective and collaborative commitment, locally and nationally, to addressing the needs of individual schools, the wider community and society.

AoEA criteria

- Criterion 6: Working in concert with the school's leadership

- Criterion 8: Understanding of causal factors impacting on school performance

- Criterion 13: Providing critical evaluation of collaborative working between governors, leaders and staff

- Criterion 14: Having an up-to-date knowledge of relevant educational policy, inspection and other related issues

Introduction

In education, the quest for improvement within schools is perpetual. It is a journey marked by multifaceted challenges, evolving methodologies and shifting paradigms. We also need to go beyond the classroom walls and into the broader context that encompasses social, economic, cultural and political dimensions. This chapter embarks on an exploration of understanding school improvement within this expansive framework.

Schools are integral parts of broader communities, and understanding the community context can help contextualise the challenges and opportunities faced by the school.

Community engagement is therefore indispensable for driving sustainable school-improvement initiatives. When schools forge strong partnerships with families, businesses, civic organisations and other community stakeholders, they can leverage collective resource, expertise and support networks to improve educational outcomes.

Moreover, community involvement fosters a sense of ownership and accountability, empowering stakeholders to actively contribute to the improvement process. By fostering a culture of collaboration and shared responsibility, schools can harness the collective wisdom and collective action of their communities to drive positive change.

Furthermore, school improvement doesn't occur in isolation. It is subject to a complex interplay of factors that span various domains. Socioeconomic conditions, cultural norms, educational policies and community dynamics all shape the landscape within which schools operate. Understanding these factors is essential for optimising effective strategies for improvement. School improvement is deeply intertwined with the fabric of society. At its core lies the aspiration to enhance educational outcomes and opportunities for all students, regardless of their backgrounds or circumstances. This pursuit is grounded in the belief that education is not merely a means to an end but a fundamental right and a cornerstone of societal progress.

The skilled education leader and adviser need to understand that there is no simple 'off-the-peg solution' for improving schools. The days of the hero school leader or professional adviser entering a school and offering a pre-packaged solution without any reference to the specific context within which the school operates are gone.

We must embark on a comprehensive examination that delves into both the intrinsic dynamics within the institution and the extrinsic forces shaping the context.

Understanding the school from within

Building from within

Before we examine the wider context, we must remind ourselves of one simple truth: schools that have built strong relationships and a clear, shared vision have a much greater chance of developing successful relationships with the external environment and communities from which their children and young people come.

The priority for anyone wishing to enable sustainable school improvement is to engage with leaders, teachers, staff members, governors and other stakeholders to gain first-hand insights into the socioeconomic and cultural norms at play within the school. The school's mission, values, goals, challenges and initiatives aimed at addressing priorities need to be seen through the eyes of those who work and live within the school's immediate and wider community.

This is particularly important when a new leader or adviser is appointed to a new school, college or education authority.

Building strong relationships

The adviser, working with the school's leadership, should assist in cultivating open, trusting and respectful relationships with teachers, staff members, students, parents and community stakeholders. These will help to provide a firm foundation on which to build and derive deeper understanding of the inner workings of the school itself. Actively listening to people's perspectives, concerns and ideas helps to demonstrate empathy and support in addressing their needs. This, in turn, will assist in enabling leadership to harness their collective strength.

'Actively listening', rather than directing, can be quite challenging for the new school leader or adviser. Often, we feel the need to demonstrate our leadership or advisory skills by suggesting or implementing change. It can be hard to hold back and not feel the need to 'prove our existence' by making quick changes, notwithstanding the fact that, on occasion, there may be a need to initiate some changes quickly.

Active listening is a crucial skill for enabling effective communication and interpersonal relationships. It aids understanding, demonstrates respect, builds trust, improves communication, fosters a productive environment and, most of all, helps the leader and adviser to learn.

Building in regular one-on-one meetings, team meetings and informal gatherings to connect with individuals and groups across the school community can all assist in strengthening rapport, sharing updates on progress, soliciting feedback and celebrating successes together.

Building and embedding a shared vision

The adviser has a role to play in supporting leadership to embed a clear and compelling vision and clarity in relation to the school's mission, goals and values in collaboration with its stakeholders. A vision that reflects the diverse perspectives and aspirations of the school's community will inspire collective commitment and ownership.

A communication of the vision regularly and transparently, emphasising the importance of collaboration, inclusivity and shared responsibility in achieving common goals, will encourage stakeholders to actively contribute to further shaping and supporting the implementation of the vision over time.

Understanding the school's learning community

The adviser, drawing on approaches advocated by the AoEA, such as Ishikawa analyses, Gemba walks and the Context for Organisational Improvement analyses, can assist leadership in understanding the school's performance and its inner workings. When done well, these can enable a deeper understanding of the school's strengths and challenges and provide a means by which improvement priorities might more holistically be addressed.

Understanding the socioeconomic context

The socioeconomic context significantly influences the educational landscape. Disparities in income, access to resources and social support systems can profoundly affect students' academic performance and opportunities. Schools situated in affluent areas may have access to greater funding, parental involvement and extracurricular opportunities, while those in disadvantaged communities often face resource constraints and tougher systemic challenges.

Addressing these disparities requires an approach that goes beyond the confines of the school walls. Collaborative efforts involving policy-makers, community organisations and educational stakeholders are essential for creating equitable opportunities and levelling the playing field for all students.

Understanding the culture

Cultural factors play a pivotal role in shaping educational practices and outcomes. Different cultures may have distinct attitudes towards education, learning styles and expectations for academic achievement. The best schools recognise and embrace diversity to create inclusive and culturally responsive learning environments. An appreciation of cultural diversity among educators is crucial for effectively engaging students from their varied backgrounds. By fostering mutual respect and understanding of all creeds and cultures, schools can cultivate an ethos that celebrates diversity as a strength, from which all can learn.

Ensuring policy is 'fit for purpose'

Education policies serve as the scaffolding upon which school improvement efforts are built. They delineate the parameters within which schools operate, assist in an allocation of resources and define expectations for student learning and achievement. However, the impact of policies on school improvement can vary widely, depending on their design, implementation and alignment with the needs of the students and communities.

Effective policy development and implementation require a nuanced understanding of how individual schools operate, local contexts, stakeholder perspectives and evidence-based practices. Policies that prioritise equity, innovation, and collaboration are more likely to catalyse meaningful change and foster a culture of continuous improvement for all who work within and with the school.

Analysing and reflecting on improvement intelligently

In the late part of the twentieth century, there was a heavy emphasis on data analysis and reflection. Academic achievement data, exam and test results, attendance records, discipline statistics and other relevant indicators to assess the school's performance were put forward as critically important in identifying areas for improvement. Disaggregating data by pupil sub-groups to identify disparities and equity gaps that require attention is, of course, important – but, on its own, quantitative data analysis is not enough. We also need to synthesise the information gathered from a much wider base. This may include research evidence, stakeholder engagement, policy analysis and community observations, in addition to the analysis of data to develop a comprehensive understanding of the societal and cultural context of the school. A good leader and adviser reflect on the interrelationships between these factors and their implications for the school and its community.

Understanding the school within its local context

There are several areas where the adviser may support the school leader in developing an understanding of the context within which a school operates locally.

Population characteristics

This involves examining the demographic data related to the school's student population, including factors such as race, ethnicity, language proficiency and special needs. Such data can provide valuable insights into the social, cultural and additional needs of the community served by the school.

Socioeconomic profiles

An investigation of the socioeconomic and demographic profiles of the school's surrounding area, including the studying of census data, economic indicators, housing patterns, employment rates and access to community resources will help to deepen an understanding of the range of financial challenges facing families.

Background history

Delving into the historical background of the school and its surrounding community might shed further light. Historical events, trends and patterns can influence present-day dynamics, including issues related to community tensions, urbanisation, immigration and economic development.

Community perspectives and concerns

It is also important to reach out to parents, guardians and family members of students enrolled in the school, particularly in matters related to significant change.

For example, when there is a proposal to change the status of a school, such as merging with another school or trust, it is considered an essential requirement to conduct surveys, establish focus groups and/or hold community meetings to solicit input on people's perspectives, concerns, aspirations and expectations regarding their children's education and the role of the school within the broader community. This degree of research and elicited communication also works best when it is part of a day-to-day approach when leading or advising a school.

Understanding the wider political context

There is also a need to understand the school within national as well as local policy frameworks.

National and local policies

National and local policies have an impact on the school's operations, funding, accountability measures, human resource guidelines and, of course, the curriculum standards expected. It is important to look at how these policies align with the school's goals and values, as well as their implications for addressing equity and access.

Political landscape

Understanding the political landscape and remaining informed by legislative developments, current debate, reforms related to education, social welfare, civil rights and other such areas can assist leaders in anticipating and planning for change.

Coming to grips with the political, social, economic and cultural context of a school involves a comprehensive approach incorporating various strategies for gathering information and insights. The AoEA advocates the use of a PESTLE analysis, where the key Political, Economic, Social, Technological, Legal and Environmental external drivers for change are considered in a systematic way for their impact on the school's development.

Avoiding working in a solitary way as a school leader is essential for fostering collaboration, innovation and collective efficacy within the school's community and across its wider system of schools. The following paragraphs offer several strategies that can help to promote a culture of collaborative improvement, and they also assist in avoiding isolation.

Actively engaging with the wider context

Encouraging collaboration

Advisers working with leaders might purposefully create structures and processes that facilitate collaboration and teamwork among teachers, staff members and other stakeholders. Collaborative planning sessions, professional learning communities, interdisciplinary projects and cross-functional teams help to foster synergy and innovation.

Providing opportunities for teachers and staff members to share expertise, resources and best practice, both within the school and with external partners, enables all to potentially benefit from one another's learning. Encouraging peer mentoring, co-teaching, lesson study and collaborative problem-solving to promote continuous improvement can facilitate some of the best professional learning and growth.

Cultivating a culture of distributed leadership where decision-making, problem-solving and innovation are shared across multiple levels of the organisation helps to systemise learning from one another. Delegating authority and responsibilities to capable individuals and teams, thus empowering them to take ownership of initiatives and contribute to school improvement efforts, strengthens capacity for sustainable improvement.

Providing leadership development opportunities, coaching and support to help emerging leaders develop their skills, confidence and capacity to lead change effectively helps to grow tomorrow's leaders from within and across a system of schools. Fostering a culture of mentorship and collaboration where experienced leaders mentor and support emerging leaders enables both the experienced and less experienced to grow together, impacting positively on the children and young people they serve.

Promoting transparent communications

Establishing clear channels of communication that facilitate open dialogue, transparency and information-sharing among all members of the school community encourages 'buy in'. Using a variety of communication methods, including staff meetings, newsletters, email updates, social media and digital platforms, to ensure information is accessible and inclusive helps to assist that information flow in a modern world.

Encouraging feedback, questions and suggestions from stakeholders demonstrates responsiveness to their input. Creating opportunities for two-way communication through surveys, focus groups, town hall meetings (where appropriate) and feedback mechanisms assists in fostering a culture of continuous improvement and mutual respect.

Collaboration with external partners

Forging partnerships with external organisations, other school providers, agencies, businesses, universities and community groups can assist in releasing resources, expertise and support for school improvement. Enabling leverage from these partnerships can assist in expanding learning opportunities, accessing funding and addressing community needs collaboratively. This may include engaging in professional networks, consortia and collaborative learning communities with other schools, districts and educational organisations to share knowledge, exchange ideas and collaborate on common challenges and goals, or participating in conferences, workshops and professional development opportunities that facilitate the cross-pollination of ideas and practices.

Addressing social media

The wider context has now become much wider! Guiding schools on the implications of social media for children is now critical. The guidance should cover comprehensive digital literacy programs that teach students critical thinking, online safety and responsible digital citizenship. There will be a need to update the curriculum to address evolving digital landscapes, education of students on the risks of cyberbullying, privacy breaches and misinformation. Collaboration with parents is vital, providing resources and workshops to foster open dialogue about the impact of social media. There will be a sustained need to develop policies promoting healthy tech habits and the monitoring of students' online activities. Ultimately, a school will need to be empowered to navigate the complex realm of social media, ensuring students harness its benefits safely.

Conclusion

By implementing such strategy informed by the school's wider context, school leaders can avoid working in a solitary way and foster a culture of collaboration, teamwork and shared leadership within the school community. By harnessing the collective wisdom, talents and energies of stakeholders, school leaders can drive meaningful change, improve student outcomes and create a positive and inclusive school culture with others.

By adopting an approach that combines research, stakeholder engagement, policy analysis, community observations and data analysis, leaders and advisers can gain a deeper understanding of the political, social, economic and cultural context of their schools. This holistic perspective will inform strategic decision-making and facilitate meaningful collaboration to address the unique needs and challenges of an individual school's community.

Sustainable school improvement needs to be seen within a wider context and requires a holistic perspective that transcends the traditional boundaries of the school itself and embraces the interconnectedness of social, cultural, economic and political factors. By recognising the nature of educational challenges and opportunities within their wider context, schools can develop more effective strategies for improvement that address the root causes of inequity, enabling all students to thrive. Ultimately, the quest for school improvement is not merely about raising test scores or meeting benchmarks; it is about creating inclusive, equitable and empowering learning environments that nurture the potential of every student and contribute to the advancement of society as a whole.

 Further reading

Darling-Hammond, L (2017) *Empowered Educators: How High-Performing Systems Shape Teacher Quality Around the World*. Hoboken, NJ: Jossey-Bass. Darling-Hammond explores the intersection of education policy, politics and social equity, emphasising the importance of considering these factors in efforts to improve educational outcomes.

Freire, P (2017) *Pedagogy of the Oppressed*. Harmondsworth: Penguin. Freire emphasises the importance of understanding the sociopolitical context in which education occurs, particularly in relation to issues of power and social context.

Fullan, M (2001) *Leading in a Culture of Change*. Hoboken, NJ: Jossey-Bass. Fullan writes about the importance of understanding broader societal contexts in education, including political and social factors.

Gardner, H (2006) *Multiple Intelligences: New Horizons in Theory and Practice*. New York: Basic Books. Gardner's work on multiple intelligences and educational theory often touches on societal and environmental influences on learning and education.

Murphy, M (2022) *Social Theory and Education Research: Understanding Foucault, Habermas, Bourdieu and Derrida*. London: Routledge. Murphy draws on the work of a wide diversity of theorists, from Dewey and Gramsci to the most recent writers who have been of particular significance to education.

2 Understanding, identifying and addressing causal factors that impact on a school's performance

TOM GRIEVESON

Key learning

- Understanding the causes of a school's performance is central to determining what needs to be done to affect its improvement.

- Knowing the context of the individual school is key. While there may be many similarities regarding why schools underperform, every school is different, with its own set of unique circumstances.

- Schools are complex organisations and their academic performance can be impacted upon by both external and internal factors, some of which the school's leaders may be able to control or influence more than others.

- Advisers working with schools can use a number of improvement tools to assist leaders in evidencing and understanding the root causes of a school's performance.

- Given the multidimensional nature of a school's performance, advisers should have a clear frame of reference within which to work so it is clear to the commissioner of the advice, the school's leadership (if different from the commissioner) and the adviser what the adviser is being asked to advise on and to what end.

AoEA criteria

- Criterion 6: Working in concert with the school's leadership

- Criterion 8: Understanding of causal factors impacting on school performance

- Criterion 9: Providing critical evaluation of performance

- Criterion 10: Providing critical evaluation of the quality of leadership

- Criterion 13: Providing critical evaluation of collaborative working between governors, leaders and staff

- Criterion 14: Having an up-to-date knowledge of relevant educational policy, inspection and other related issues

Introduction

Schools are complex organisations with academic performance influenced by a myriad of external and internal factors:

> *Calls to understand what works in education are made the world over. We need to know not only what 'works' but under what conditions, how and why. Causation is central to this. Researchers, educationalists and users of research need to know the effects of causes and the causes of effects.*
>
> (Morrison, 2009)

Unpicking the intricate interchange between the various causal factors requires us to explore the concept of causation in more depth. In doing so, we will examine the connections between different variables and their respective contributions. We must also differentiate between correlation and causation; we are not seeking association, but rather what is directly causing things to be the way they are.

What might these causes include? The answers include demographics, teaching quality, the appropriateness of the curriculum on offer, students' interactions with each other and staff and much else besides. Untangling the complex relationships at play in any school will require leaders and those who support them to be forensic in searching for the evidence to better understand where the causal chains are located.

This chapter is intended to be practical; we will use two key tools advocated by the AoEA that have proved to be helpful in the quest to ascertain causation in a school's performance. These are:

- *force field analysis*, used with the knowledge of the school to identify positive and negative forces at play;
- *Ishikawa analysis*, to assist in identifying likely causes and provide the basis for evidence-gathering in relation to a particular area of underperformance.

Each of these models is used regularly by AoEA colleagues and they have proved consistently helpful in enabling schools to successfully address often seemingly impenetrable challenges. We will take a step-by-step approach, introducing the use of each tool matched to a real school example. The AoEA has produced an online training module to support colleagues to further amplify how these approaches can work.

Schools are busy places and staff are constantly facing daily challenges. Often, when advisers are asked to help, it is because leaders require additional capacity to support their work. They will have already tried to address issues themselves but may have been overwhelmed by the day-to-day tsunami of matters confronting them. The following is a real school example. An external and highly experienced adviser and a LA colleague worked closely with the school's leadership to support its efforts to resolve the difficulties faced.

Example school context

The example school is a large, 1500-student secondary school serving a particularly challenging local context with high student mobility and a high degree of social deprivation. More than 50 per cent of students are entitled to a free school meal, although not all families take up the offer. The school is a beacon for many families, with extensive support networks operating within the school, including social services and medical drop-in facilities. Staff turnover is relatively high, particularly among middle leaders, so temporary acting positions in the school are commonplace. The principal is due to retire in a few months along with one of two deputies. Governors have not been able to recruit to the principal post, although a new deputy principal will start within the next month. The local authority has secured a two-year secondment of an experienced principal from a school elsewhere in the borough. The school has also attracted new leadership positions in English and mathematics, although new colleagues will not start until the beginning of the new academic year. Student attendance levels following the COVID-19 pandemic are still too low, with high persistent absence rates. Education welfare support is limited. Academic achievement has declined across several indicators, including the recognised, expected standard 4+ and 5+ GCSE in English and mathematics at age 16. Both departments currently have temporary leadership and neither is being supported directly by a member of the senior leadership team. Performance across the EBacc range of subjects (English, mathematics, sciences, humanities and a modern foreign language) is variable, and science and technology outcomes in particular are low.

Throughout this worked example, you will note the emphasis on collaborative working to understand the potential causes of underperformance more fully.

- *Collaborative working*. The tools used in this example work best if there is collaboration so that a range of views can be considered. In this case, senior and middle leaders were present as well as a group of the governing body and a LA representative of this local authority-maintained school. The seconded principal and a highly experienced external adviser were also present. A questionnaire seeking the views of staff and students was made available. This approach limited the likelihood of 'groupthink', which can occur when there is a desire for group harmony, in order to prioritise consensus over critical analysis. Irving Janis (2008) uses the term 'groupthink' to refer to a way of thinking that people engage in when looking for agreement in group discussion becomes so dominant that it overrides a realistic appraisal of possible alternative courses of action.

- *Systematising the process*. Using the tools outlined above to provide structure and a clear pathway.

- *The use of verifiable evidence*. 'Hunches' and 'bright ideas' often provide a good starting point for exploring an issue, but they must be underpinned by evidence if we are to successfully identify the causal chains that will lead us to the underlying causes of the

was to be addressed. Each group outlined its road map of what should be done and how this could be achieved. Each presentation showed some overlap with each of the other three areas, and a member from each team then worked with the challenge group to produce a completed and coherent plan.

Conclusion

Taking the time with leaders and governors at the outset to 'dig deep' in determining the principal causes of underperformance, along with the related actions to address these, laid the foundation for the school to remain sharply focused on the right priorities. A marked improvement in leadership capacity in mathematics and science has, within a short space of time, impacted on the quality of provision and produced better results for almost all groups of learners at GCSE. Internal assessment, borne out by external validation and scrutiny, indicates that other subjects are on track for a similar result, with improved capacity in senior and middle leadership impacting positively on curriculum design, well-targeted professional learning and pedagogical practice. School-based research and evaluation of practice are helping to inform the next best steps. While challenges remain, the school's own expectation of itself is greater, leaders are more sharply focused on their core function and the school is on a journey of well-informed continuous improvement.

Further reading

Janis, I L (2008) *IEEE Engineering Management Review*, 36.

Tahir, U (2019) Lewin's Force Field Analysis (Change Management). Available at: https://changemanagementinsight.com/lewins-force-field-analysis-change-management (accessed 28 May 2024).

Wikipedia (2024) The Ishikawa Diagram. *Wikipedia*. Available at: https://en.wikipedia.org/wiki/Ishikawa_diagram (accessed 29 May 2024).

References

Brown, C, Schildkamp, K and Hubers, M D (2017) Combining the Best of Two Worlds: A Conceptual Proposal for Evidence-informed School Improvement. *Educational Research*, 59(2): 154–72. https://doi.org/10.1080/00131881.2017.1304327

Morrison, K (2009) *Causation in Educational Research*, London: Routledge. Quote from online book abstract. [online] Available at: www.amazon.co.uk/Causation-Educational-Research-Keith-Morrison/dp/0415496497 (accessed 23 August 2024).

Organisation for Economic Co-operation and Development [OECD] (2017) The Welsh Education Reform Journey: A Rapid Policy Assessment. Available at: www.oecd.org/education/thewelsheducationreformjourneyarapidpolicyassessment.htm (accessed 28 May 2024).

Slavin, R E (2020) How Evidence-based Reform will Transform Research and Practice in Education. *Educational Psychologist*, 55(1): 21–31. https://doi.org/10.1080/00461520.2019.1611432 (accessed on 28/05/24)

Tahir, U (2019) Lewin's Force Field Analysis (Change Management). Available at: https://changemanagementinsight.com/lewins-force-field-analysis-change-management (accessed 28 May 2024).

Wikipedia (2024) The Ishikawa Diagram. *Wikipedia*. Available at: https://en.wikipedia.org/wiki/Ishikawa_diagram (accessed 29 May 2024).

3 Marginal gains: school improvement approaches that build on success and assist in addressing educational equity

REBECCA JACKSON

Key learning

- Substantial change takes time, energy and commitment; keep on keeping on.

- Staff, children, governors and families need to be aware of the reasons behind the changes; explain the 'why'.

- Share the good news as it happens; communicate with your community.

AoEA criteria

- Criterion 6: Working in concert with the school's leadership

- Criterion 8: Understanding of causal factors impacting on school performance

- Criterion 9: Providing critical evaluation of performance

- Criterion 11: Providing critical evaluation of the quality of teaching

- Criterion 12: Providing critical evaluation of pastoral provision

Introduction

In this chapter, I will share how my experience as an education adviser enabled me to critically analyse the context of a school and work with the staff and community to ensure greater equity in the school's educational offering. It is a tale of marginal gains and slow improvements rather than quick wins and rapid change. I suggest that this approach could be replicated elsewhere by advisers and school leaders looking to minimise the impact of poverty on the children and young people in their care.

Addressing the impact of poverty on children and families: a school improvement case study

The Joseph Rowntree Foundation (2024) report states that 25 per cent of children in the North-East of England are now living in poverty and offers several recommendations to address this growing crisis. It is my belief that schools play a vital role as part of the wider solution. In this chapter, I will explain how one school tackled the challenge of creating greater educational equity. Before outlining the actions taken by the school, however, I suggest we define our terms and in doing so I acknowledge the contribution to the debate made by Lee Elliott Major (2024), who proposes that instead of the more commonly used phrase 'disadvantaged pupils', we use the phrase 'children from under resourced backgrounds'. He argues that '*this is to avoid the trap of deficit thinking. The deficit approach frames certain children as somehow inferior*'.

School overview

The case study school is a large primary school in the North-East of England with 418 children on roll. Thirteen per cent of these are children from under-resourced backgrounds; 15 per cent are children with English as an additional language; 9 per cent are children with special educational needs and disabilities (SEND). The school has 13 ethnic groups and there are 22 languages spoken in the children's homes.

The school was judged outstanding in 2014. It has a stable workforce and school population, and a committed and hard-working staff team. However, the school data relating to behaviour, attendance and attainment revealed a discrepancy between those children eligible for Pupil Premium and their peers. However, this was not just a data issue; staff and governors were also driven by a strong commitment to the school family to leaving no one behind, removing any potential barriers that may result from poverty. Every week in assembly, children and staff come together to say the school promise, which begins with the words, *'This is our school and we are a family. Let us promise that we will love each other as brothers and sisters.'* The school wants to ensure this promise is visible in all aspects of school life.

The adviser, school staff and governors worked together on a ten-step plan to improve outcomes for children from under resourced families. While not exhaustive, this list could be adapted and used by advisers/ school leaders in any school looking to create a more equitable offering.

Ten steps towards a more equitable education

1. Identify barriers

The starting point for this work was to identify and then systematically attempt to remove any barriers that were inhibiting the ability of children to fully participate in school life. A 'Poverty Proofing' audit was commissioned to be undertaken by Children North East. Poverty Proofing the School Day is a powerful tool for identifying the barriers faced by children living in poverty when it comes to engaging fully with school life and its opportunities. Focused on listening to the voices and experiences of young people, it offers a pathway for schools to address often unseen inequalities within their activities, helping them to reduce stigma, break the link between educational attainment and financial background, and support schools to explore the most effective way to spend Pupil Premium.

2. Plan actions

The audit resulted in a report that highlighted areas of strength as well as areas for improvement. An action plan was written and this was shared with governors, families, children and staff. SLT led information sessions for governors as well as information/training sessions for families.

3. Re-examine annual events

The action plan suggested making changes to key annual events to make them easily accessible to all. Admission charges to all Parents, Teachers and Friends Association (PTFA)/school events were immediately removed. Other changes to these events were also necessary: the 'Christmas fair' fundraiser became the 'Winter festival', an after-school event where most activities were free. The Summer Fayre was redesigned so many activities were free and the refreshment stall became *'pay as you feel'*. World Book Day became World Book Week, a time to celebrate books and reading across the school instead of a day of dressing up. 'Toy Day' became an afternoon where staff played games with the children and shared stories and snacks. These seemingly small adjustments remove potential barriers and so enable more families to participate in school life, should they want to, rather than preventing them from being part of the school community by putting a pricing barrier in the way.

4. Ensure consistency

As well as the changes that were made to whole-school annual events, issues related to the management of learning and learning behaviours were found to be in need of review. There was an acknowledgement that some of the most vulnerable children were falling through the gaps created by the inconsistencies that existed across the school. So the adviser, SLT and school staff looked at ways to ensure consistency in all areas and across all key stages. There were three areas of focus: curriculum, interventions and behaviour.

Curriculum

Enriching texts and experiences were put at the heart of all learning and careful whole-school planning ensured progression for all. The curriculum was constructed to be *'irresistible to all learners'*.

Interventions

Historically, a vast range of interventions have been delivered across the school in a myriad of ways. This was reduced to a core 'suite' of interventions and learning support assistants were trained in delivering these interventions. Quality rather than quantity became the focus.

Behaviour

While behaviour was generally good in the school, there was no cohesive approach across all age groups. The 'Thrive approach' was implemented as it provided a clear framework upon which to build. Behaviour across the school improved and, just as importantly, children were supported in ways that best met their behavioural and emotional needs.

5. Increase family support

Marc Rowlands (2015) and the Education Endowment Fund (2023) recommend that some of the Pupil Premium funding should be spent on wider services, including supporting families. A family support worker and an art psychotherapist were recruited and quickly became an integral part of the school staff team.

6. Reframe attendance management

While the school continues to acknowledge the positive impact of good attendance, it understands that attendance is often an adult-led rather than a child-led issue, and families are supported via our education welfare officer. Staff work with parents and carers in families for whom attendance is an issue rather than shaming the children whose attendance is low. There are no longer celebrations for 100 per cent attendance and there are no league tables of attendance class by class.

7. Enable equal access to extracurricular activities

Most extracurricular clubs are run by staff and are free. Many clubs run at lunchtime, ensuring that children who wish to attend the clubs are able to do so. Children eligible for Pupil Premium access receive residential visits at a significantly reduced, or no cost and with payment plans in place.

8. Uniform

Both the school and PE uniform are 'low cost' and easy to purchase. There is also a thriving secondhand uniform offer run by the PTFA.

9. Upskill governors

SLT-led briefing sessions for governors on the effective use of Pupil Premium funding, as it is essential that governors both support and understand this area of school development and the associated spending plans. Governor recruitment – another important tool – has been used to support the momentum of school development.

10. Think about your language

There is a risk in defining children as 'Pupil Premium children' as this group of children is not homogeneous – and it is dangerous to treat them as such. Therefore, the school now consistently uses the phrase 'children eligible for Pupil Premium' rather than 'Pupil Premium children'. The school requested that Children North East also use this phrase in the report it produced. The researchers corrected the language used on the report and Children North East now uses 'children eligible for Pupil Premium' rather than 'Pupil Premium children' in all its reports.

Like all schools in England, the case study school has to report on the spending of Pupil Premium via the government pro-forma. The pro-forma was adapted to ensure that it worked for the school and reflected the approach being taken regarding children eligible for Pupil Premium. Instead of listing the possible challenges facing children eligible for Pupil Premium, the school cited the challenges facing the school in the quest to enable all children to succeed. These questions may be helpful starting points for other advisers/school leaders when deciding on how to use Pupil Premium.

- How can we sustain outstanding teaching and learning for all our children?

- How do we retain and develop our high-quality staff?

- What strategies can we employ to ensure the social and emotional well-being of our children?

- How can we ensure that the progress of all children is robustly monitored and leads to impactful interventions?

- How can we ensure that interventions are streamlined, consistent and impactful?
- How can we ensure we have a rich and ambitious curriculum?

In the Pupil Premium strategy document, the school outlines how spending helps to address these issues.

Conclusion

The school has been working to establish greater equity in its school offering for over five years. Despite the pandemic, data relating to children eligible for Pupil Premium suggest an improving picture. Moreover, anecdotal and qualitative evidence points to a more inclusive school where all children and their families are increasingly able to access everything the school has to offer. This quote drives the work and can be seen on the office walls of senior leaders: *'Schools, in their structure and organisation, can do more than simply reflect the society we have; they can try to be precursor of the kind of society that we wish to have'* (Gorard, 2010, p 48).

 Further reading

Children North East (2023) Available at: https:// children-ne.org.uk/ poverty-proofing-the-school-day (accessed 15 May 2024).

UK Government (2023) *Pupil Premium Strategy Statement Template*. Available at: www.gov.uk/ government/publications/pupil-premium (accessed 29 June 2024).

UK Government (2023) *Schools, Pupils and Their Characteristics, Academic Year 2022/23*. Available at: https://explore-education-statistics.service.gov.uk/find-statistics/school-pupils-and-their-characteristics (accessed 14 May 2024).

References

Education Endowment Fund (2023) https://educationendowmentfoundation.org.uk/guidance-for-teachers/using-pupil-premium (accessed 15 May 2024).

Elliott Major, L (2024) Why We Need to Stop Talking About Disadvantage (and What We Should Talk About Instead). *Schools Week*. Available at: https://schoolsweek.co.uk/why-we-need-to-stop-talking-about-disadvantage-and-what-we-should-talk-about-instead (accessed 29 June 2024).

Gorard, S (2010) Education Can Compensate for Society – a Bit. *British Journal of Educational Studies*, 58(1): 47–65.

Joseph Rowntree Foundation (2024) *UK Poverty 2024: The Essential Guide to Understanding Poverty in the UK*. London: Joseph Rowntree Foundation.

Rowlands, M (2015) *An Updated Guide to the Pupil Premium*. Wakefield: Charlesworth Press.

4 Supporting new headteachers in identifying their priorities within an effective induction programme

STUART ADLAM

Key learning

- Newly appointed headteachers benefit from support to familiarise themselves with the wider context of their school, ideally brokered at the point of recruitment.

- External advisers can provide valuable support through a review of the school's context, supporting school self-evaluation and building a robust programme of school improvement.

- The provision of an experienced headteacher mentor for new headteachers is the least structured but potentially one of the most important aspects of an effective induction programme.

- Opportunities for new headteachers to work together to share their experiences of early headship, and to develop practice through collaborative reflection and problem-solving, are an essential component of effective induction.

- There is an argument that some aspects of induction and training are best delivered once the newly appointed headteacher has completed their first year and has a deeper understanding of their school's context.

AoEA criteria

- Criterion 6: Working in concert with the school's leadership

- Criterion 9: Providing critical evaluation of performance

- Criterion 10: Providing critical evaluation of the quality of leadership

- Criterion 11: Providing critical evaluation of the quality of teaching

- Criterion 12: Providing critical evaluation of pastoral provision

- Criterion 13: Providing critical evaluation of collaborative working between governors, leaders and staff

Introduction

As the school improvement and advisory service for Hampshire Local Authority, we work in partnership with over 500 maintained early years, primary, secondary and special schools across the local authority. In our maintained schools, we are actively engaged with governing bodies in the appointment and subsequent induction of newly appointed headteachers – typically 20 or more new headteachers annually. The profile of newly appointed headteachers remains very varied across the local authority, with colleagues joining our schools with wide-ranging experiences and career paths, including those with multiple previous headships.

In my experience, the induction process for newly appointed headteachers has required refinement and renewal to meet the changing needs of new headteachers and the contexts of their schools, particularly post-pandemic. This chapter outlines some of the main changes we have made to the induction process and how they have been developed and refined over time, through working with school improvement colleagues, governors and, importantly, newly appointed headteachers themselves. While some of the features of this process have stood the test of time, reviews undertaken by Derek Myers, School Improvement Manager (HIAS), have significantly shaped our most recent changes.

The induction process

Ideally, the induction of new headteachers will be commissioned by governors or the responsible body as part of the recruitment process and in the context of the support and training that have already been discussed with the new headteacher. If this is the case, you will already have a good understanding of the new headteacher's professional development needs. If not, then an initial meeting with the newly appointed headteacher and governors will be essential to broker a successful programme.

It is important to note that even if the newly appointed headteacher has previous headship experience, they are not yet experienced in their new context and will need your support to understand which of their headship experiences and skills are transferrable, which are not and where their professional skills and knowledge will require further development.

Increasingly, the challenges and demands of headship post-pandemic require an effective induction, which provides bespoke support and challenge, to ensure the newly appointed headteacher is successful enough in their first year. The challenges of a publicly high profile and accountable role can fit the old saying, 'if at first you don't succeed, you don't succeed!'

In our experience, a successful headteacher induction programme typically comprises four complementary strands that are designed to meet the induction needs of new headteachers:

1. familiarisation, sharing key information and building wider organisational relationships;
2. a review of the school's context, supporting school self-evaluation and a programme of school improvement;
3. a new headteacher mentor;
4. new headteacher networks.

All these elements provide a key element of effective induction that will support, develop and empower new headteachers to lead their schools successfully.

Strand 1: Familiarisation, sharing key information and building wider organisational relationships

This strand will reflect the particular context of the school and is an opportunity to explore the vison, values and ethos of the wider school community, whether it be a local authority or multi-academy trust. As a large local authority, we facilitate familiarisation meetings where new headteachers are briefed by senior local authority officers, who discuss key themes that will shape the work of the new headteacher. These themes will typically include local authority priorities (such as improving attendance), safeguarding and provision for vulnerable groups.

Whether leading a local authority, a maintained school, a stand-alone academy or as part of a multi-academy trust, sharing important information about the services and support available, as well as key contacts and roles, is essential to help a new headteacher to navigate the wider context in which they are working. For example, to support the process of information sharing and relationship-building, we provide a series of new headteacher webinars. These provide opportunities for colleagues who provide services and support to schools to brief headteachers and answer questions. The webinars can be live-streamed or pre-recorded, depending on the local context. Currently our webinars include:

- Education Finance Services, Education Personnel Services, Governor Services;

- Primary Behaviour Service, Inclusion Support Service, SEND;

- Safeguarding, LADOs, Health and Safety;

- Assessment, Early Career Teachers, EYFS;

- Support from subject advisers (all curriculum subjects).

In our experience, the webinar element of the new headteacher induction programme has greatly reduced the need to share large amounts of information at the familiarisation meetings and provides more time for the important work of leadership development and school improvement.

Strand 2: A review of the school's context, supporting school self-evaluation and a programme of school improvement

This strand of headteacher induction is designed to support the new headteacher to identify and deliver on key school improvement priorities and provide bespoke training, guidance and support. Ideally, the review will be commissioned by the governing body, or responsible body, as part of the recruitment process and will involve an adviser who has supported the recruitment process and knows the school.

The review is also an opportunity for the adviser to provide ongoing personalised professional development and advice around key challenges faced by new headteachers – for example, getting the pace of change right, selecting the right priorities to address initially and 'picking your battles', which all require a steady guiding hand and sage advice. Similarly, building effective relationships with key stakeholders including senior colleagues, the chair of governors and the governing board and other professional partners can be problematic in the early weeks and months of headship and review activities provide an opportunity for the adviser to model and guide around these themes.

The focus of the review might be shaped by the key tasks identified by the governors as part of the recruitment process or as the result of subsequent school self-evaluation and the new headteacher's initial analysis of the school. It is likely that priorities will include providing critical evaluation of the quality of leadership, the quality of teaching and pastoral provision. The best practice involves working alongside the new headteacher and helping them to draw appropriate insights from what can be a highly complex early engagement. There are times when the skill of the adviser is to underline and reinforce the new headteacher's perceptions. At other times, it can be to sensitively challenge overly critical or under-evidenced impressions. It is often easier for new headteachers to identify weaknesses and areas requiring development than to fully appreciate the school's existing strengths and how and why the school has developed its approaches to provision. As such, there is a risk of inadvertently undoing or neglecting effective practice. Helping the headteacher to gain a balanced and accurate insight through supported self-evaluation will be the starting point of the review.

The initial meeting in the headteacher review process should also look at the wider school context, including the local authority's or trust's view of priorities and any related reports. In our maintained schools, we would also consider any local authority support package, its impact so far and whether any further support is needed from the school improvement team, governor services, finance and so on. Similarly, identifying where the school is in the Ofsted inspection cycle, and sense checking the headteacher's and school's readiness if the school is within the inspection window, would also be key considerations.

Developing a positive professional working relationship with the school's governance body is critical to a new headteacher's first year. The challenge can be that governors are already moulded into working practices from the previous incumbent headteacher. Changes in approaches, communication styles and expectations on both sides can be tricky. The role of the adviser is to help the headteacher and, if possible, the governing body to understand the implications and potential benefits of change and at times its necessity.

The adviser can facilitate the review process in many ways, although it is probably best undertaken as a series of half-day school visits over the course of the new headteacher's first year. Once the initial evaluation is completed, key focus areas should be agreed, and a plan co-constructed with the headteacher and agreed with the governing body. In our local authority context, these priorities would be summarised in a New Headteacher Review Plan, with agreed time scales, school improvement activities, term milestones and clear objectives. Coaching, training and support are provided by the adviser during subsequent visits and the review process itself becomes an ongoing professional inquiry and dialogue between the headteacher and the adviser. The process should have sufficient flexibility to adapt to the new headteacher's professional development needs and any changes in the school's context.

At the end of the review process, a meeting between the adviser and the headteacher and chair of governors provides an opportunity to share the outcomes of the review. Importantly, it is also an opportunity to identify any additional professional development needs and agree any further support.

Strand 3: Headteacher mentor

The provision of an experienced headteacher mentor for new headteachers is the least-structured but potentially one of the most important aspects of an effective induction programme. Finding the right match is important and requires a high degree of professional judgement and knowledge of both the mentor and mentee; it should also consider the preferences of the new headteacher. Our experience has shown that, ideally, mentors should not be too local as this can impair objectivity and risk conflicts of interests. However, some similarities in the type, size and demographics of the respective schools can be an advantage.

As a voluntary role that relies on the professional generosity of experienced headteachers, some training for headteacher mentors is highly beneficial to ensure they are prepared for the potential challenges and pitfalls. The role is to advise and guide, and act as a professional friend, so the need for confidentiality should be balanced with the availability of advice and support for mentors, ideally from an adviser. This relationship, after initial mentor training and once established, is managed by the headteacher and mentor, and often develops into a collaboration that extends well beyond the first year of induction. There are, of course, times where the match is not made in heaven and either fails to establish or breaks down irreparably. As such, regular opportunities for advisers to touch base with mentors and mentees are advisable so advice and guidance can be provided and, where necessary, a change of horses facilitated.

Strand 4: New headteacher networks

Opportunities for new headteachers to work together to share their experiences of early headship, and to develop practice through collaborative reflection and problem-solving, are an essential component of effective induction. Education advisers are potentially well placed to develop and facilitate networks for new headteachers that provide structured opportunities for peer support and development. As a large local authority, we can pump-prime this process through a two-day annual conference for new headteachers. This provides scope to both explore key aspects of headship with a new headteacher and establish and build professional relationships with other new headteachers that will provide emotional and developmental support well beyond the induction period. In recent years, our cohorts of new headteachers have established private social media groups to facilitate ongoing contact and communication, as a hub for problem-solving and information-seeking, and as a means of commissioning further training and support.

We know from experience that core aspects of headship, including instructional leadership, school improvement and school self-evaluation, are potentially at risk from the other pressures of early headship. The opportunity for new headteachers to come together, ideally with an adviser or senior colleagues to work in groups, is an essential component of their induction, which helps them to refocus away from operational pressure and consider more strategic aspects of the role.

To this end, our conference and networking opportunities provide structured opportunities to problem-solve school-specific issues with colleagues and to consider and explore the principles of effective strategic leadership. We provide regular opportunities to share best practice including presentations from established, high-performing headteachers. Principles of effective school improvement, including monitoring, review and evaluation, are explored in detail and we ensure a strong focus on instructional leadership, as this can easily be neglected by new headteachers in the first year of headship.

Supporting new headteachers beyond the first year

Our work with newly appointed headteachers and the findings of recent research are now shaping our thinking about their training needs beyond the first year of induction.

There is an argument that some aspects of induction and training are best delivered once the newly appointed headteacher has completed their first year and has a deeper understanding of their school's context. Our work with experienced headteachers has also informed our thinking around the induction process. Recent local authority training for experienced headteachers (Five Fundamentals of Effective School Leadership), designed to revisit and explore some of the fundamental aspects of school improvement and school leadership post-COVID, has highlighted a need for regular leadership training for headteachers beyond the first year of headship and is echoed in policy implications from recent research:

> - *Enhancing the quality of school leadership may be a cost-effective way of improving school performance and more work should be done on how to achieve it.*
>
> - *School governors and Ofsted inspectors should acknowledge that it may take years to realise the full improvement in results from switching headteachers and support new headteachers accordingly.*
>
> - *Effective headteachers significantly improve pupil attainment, teacher retention and teacher absenteeism.*
>
> (Zuccollo et al, 2023, p 4)

We know from research that effective headteachers positively impact on school performance outcomes for pupils and that leadership improvement programmes beyond the induction year make an important contribution to headteacher effectiveness. We are now planning a training offer for the second and third years of headship that explores further some of the fundamental building blocks of successful leadership. The programme will include:

- managing school self-evaluation and school improvement;

- the pupil progress review process;

- leading the development of high-quality inclusive teaching, including well-designed programmes of CPD;

- curriculum leadership;

- layered leadership for school improvement.

We recognise that there are many other key elements of effective school leadership that could be included; however, we believe these five areas are critical for effective headship and school improvement.

Conclusion

Importantly, as education advisers, we should be viewing headteacher induction as the start of a process of support and development that continues deep into headship. We should be aiming to continue to provide high-quality professional learning that will equip newly appointed headteachers with the skills, professional knowledge and expertise they will continue to need in their second year of headship and beyond:

> *Our findings suggest that enhancing the quality of school leadership may be an effective means of improving school performance, provided that an effective approach to enhancing it can be identified. Although leadership improvement programmes already exist, our work underscores the need to evaluate their impact and ensure that they are effective, given the high potential payoff for good leadership development.*
>
> (Zuccollo et al, 2023, p 25)

 Further reading

Zuccollo, J, Cardim Dias, J, Jimenez, E and Braakmaan, N (2023) *The Influence of Headteachers on Their Schools.* London: Education Policy Institute.

5 Owning improvement: 'Tá gach lá ina lá scoile'

MAIRÉAD MHIG UAID

Key learning

- *'Tá gach lá ina lá scoile'* – it is important to believe that *'every day is a school day'* and that the collective, focused efforts of individuals learning and improving brings improvement.

- This chapter demonstrates the primacy of each of us:

  - being a learner

  - knowing what we want to achieve as a collective

  - aligning our day-to-day focus with that shared vision and purpose.

AoEA criteria

- Criterion 6: Working in concert with the school's leadership

- Criterion 8: Understanding of causal factors impacting on school performance

- Criterion 14: Having an up-to-date knowledge of relevant educational policy and other related issues

Introduction

This chapter is an opportunity to reflect on almost 30 years working and advising in Northern Ireland, mainly within Irish Medium Education (IME) and more recently within English Medium Education (EME). I believe the purpose of education is to make the world an inclusive, peaceful space of shared prosperity and that through addressing the factors that have led to our current best, we can create that state. This chapter focuses on improvement through the intentional, collective application of time and energy.

Owning improvement: reflecting

For most of its pupils in this jurisdiction, IME is delivered as immersion education; pupils live through one language at school and another at home. In IME, Irish is the language of the school, and while English is the predominant language of homes, the home language could be any language. For significant numbers of its pupils, Irish is the language of both home and school. In IME, pupils become bi-literate in Irish and English.

IME came to life in Belfast in 1971 when a group of committed parents established what became the '*bunscoil*' (IME primary school), the first of its kind in Northern Ireland; within the monolingual EME system, the curriculum would be delivered in Irish, and their own and others' children would grow as a community of Irish-speaking families. Wages were paid via collections and donations (Bunscoil Phobal Feirste, 2024); the founders' determination to realising their vision was mirrored by community support. A perfect example of vision to reality, the vision became reality because all its people made that vision their day-to-day reality. Everybody did what they could do to the best of their ability to support it. It is a perfect example of addressing factors that affect the desired end result, through collaborative, focused effort. The *result* is the *product* of what *every one* of us chooses to *focus* on, of how we choose to spend our *time* and our *energy*:

$$\text{Result} = \text{Everyone} \times (\text{Focus} \times \text{Time} \times \text{Energy})$$

The reality in our system today, and its outworking – the reality of what we get and what we currently have – is the result of our collective endeavour to date. Improvement on that result happens when we consciously choose to learn, to improve and focus our time and energy differently as a unit for the greater collective good. Sustainable improvement is the slow, dedicated, focused endeavour of the many.

Owning improvement: learning

By the mid-1990s, when I began to teach, numerous more IME schools had opened across the region. That early vision was already superseded and, through widespread focus, time and energy, today IME is supported by legislation (Northern Ireland Office, 1998), an informed IME curriculum (CCEA, 2009) and a wider range of IME resources. There are 45 nursery settings, 35 primary settings and five post-primary settings (CnaG, 2020).

A tangible manifestation of identity, language is a uniquely motivating factor. IME schools are an amplification of that, and increased discretionary effort has therefore been its norm. As an IME primary school leader, I became used to doing extra voluntarily, as many practitioners have done. For example, I taught full-time for most of my school-based career. Tailored language-specific planning and resource preparation, safeguarding, developing an active ethos of inclusive school improvement and other responsibilities were fulfilled before the pupils came in, when they went home or occasionally when release time was available. At that time, modern-day immersion education was a fledgling movement globally, and being in class facilitated my research and evidence-based approach. My focus, necessitated by context, was on learning and improving upon my own practice, and on leading, supporting and advising others as they improved theirs. Providing high-quality teaching and learning in immersion education has added layers of competency, namely expertise in immersion language and literacy pedagogy, linguistic skill and the capacity to track and articulate undefined development with confidence. I sought to develop each of these concurrently.

My practice in class and in school led to advisory work at the sectoral level in the creation of IME immersion literacy resources and guidance, and IME SEN guidance, as well as their associated teacher professional learning. Further, it led to deepened sectoral and system understanding of and advocacy for IME inclusion and its SEN provision. In IME, it is quite normal for school staff to focus their time and energy so that their practice informs sectoral development regionally and across Ireland, and at the same time informs understanding of IME within the wider Northern Ireland education system. The result is collective: enriched and increased societal use of Irish, and a wider appreciation of our shared past and our shared present. The Focus for Improvement model in Figure 5.1 represents such conscious improvement, where the day-to-day operational and organisational improvement work in education has the knock-on effect of societal improvement. Each stage feeds into the next, consciously improving and re-improving that wider societal footprint.

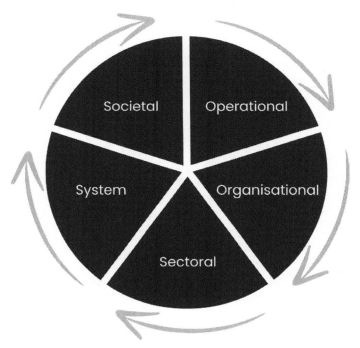

Figure 5.1: Focus for Improvement model

Owning improvement: advising

Within that context of school and sectoral development, I matured as an adviser. Through experience, research, reading and application, I learned about values and principles, about responsibility and accountability. I learned that whatever the factors and focus may be, the one and only thing I can control is myself, as Covey's (1989) Circle of Concern/Circle of Influence model explains. That learning and experience keeps me 'in lane' as an adviser. The more I improve myself – my skills and knowledge and the way I respond – the greater influence I can have on those I advise or collaborate with, and the greater the momentum and change we can bring together. The first step towards improving anything begins with that deep understanding, coupled with an intrinsic desire to know better, to do better, to be better and to believe that such investment is worthwhile.

Consider young children. They are abundantly inquisitive and passionate to learn and do new things for themselves, to have fun. They have an intrinsic, self-directed desire to learn and achieve, a *'no one else can do this for me'* approach. As learners improving, we must know and value what makes us 'tick' and make our work and learning enjoyable. The Influencing Change model in Figure 5.2 is my approach to advising on school and system improvement.

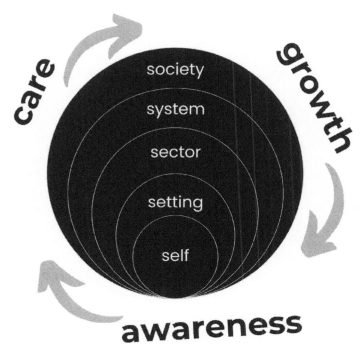

Figure 5.2: Influencing Change model

On an individual level, I must in the first instance want to improve. I must have sufficient self-awareness to know that my best in 2020 should be different from and better than my best in 2010. I must care about improving, about doing better for myself and about doing better for all the people who are impacted on by my work. Within my work, I must know what I am good at, and be able to pinpoint one thing I want to improve upon that will make me better at what I do. Through targeted resolve, I can learn, I can apply my learning and I can make that an enjoyable experience. Improvement doesn't diminish from my previous bests. It simply acknowledges that my investment in myself is worthwhile.

I can become increasingly self-aware, and I can regulate a paced balance of this growth with care. In doing so, I model and nurture this as a way of being. In extending my self-awareness and openness to work with, and to learn from, a wider range of people, I improve how I do what I do. Each improved version of me improves my response to my work remit.

As an adviser to others, and within my current organisation, I can coach, teach, advise or influence from my experience and learning. I can pace focused setting improvement sensitively in line with the organisation's current context, tailored to individual staff need. I can trust that I am making the right decisions with staff that raise their capacity to improve. Through fun and gentle reflection, staff can consider how and to what extent they operate in line with their own need for care and growth and how and to what extent they operate in line with their own values. From that self-reflection and self-awareness, they can identify one small thing to improve upon, to commit to and to do better. For example, if my most deeply held value is 'respect', what is my contribution to our ethos? What are my exact behaviours to colleagues or children which show them respect? What behaviour can I improve upon that deepens this respect? What is my contribution to improving the quality of teaching and learning? What does respect look like in provision for pupils, in my leadership style, in how I have accessed professional learning to improve my teaching? How am I committing to growing as a teacher or as a leader and what informs that? How can I measure my own improvement? Sustainable improvement is a commitment to the self in the first instance.

Dedicated learning, commitment to improving one seemingly small focus and recognising success lead to empowerment and to choosing to commit to a cycle of collective improvement.

As we are more aware of how we care for and grow ourselves, we better inform our individual practice. When each person within a setting is a self-directed self-improver, through agreed and shared focus they can energise real change collectively. Collective setting or system improvement doesn't diminish from our previous bests; it simply acknowledges that our application and investment in ourselves is worthwhile. When groups of settings operate through collective agreed focus, they can activate improvement across the systems that affect them. Systems that are informed by society improve society, celebrate diversity, equity and inclusion, and sustain our space and peace.

The Influencing Change model is indicative of the foundation and development of IME regionally: self-aware, self-directed individuals aligning their day-to-day focus with their collective, longer-term vision of what they want for their children, harnessing their awareness, care and growth to make their vision a reality. Setting improvement, sectoral and system improvement and societal improvement are the product of self-aware, self-directed individuals focusing on the same end result. Through collective, intentional desire and endeavour, we can create our shared vision using the resources already available to us and already invested in us.

Owning improvement: refining

In recent years, there has been great urgency to measure efficacy of and improvement in education through the metrics of literacy and numeracy rather than through the desirability of education as a career or efficacy of or improvement in society. When sustainable improvement happens, there is a personal and a collective recognition that improvement is a core function of the self, that it is not a static, one-off event and that it is not something a new colleague will do. It is not something an outside entity comes in to do for the setting. It is of the self and it is of the setting.

Conclusion

Sustainable school and system improvement happens when there is a collective recognition of the importance of improving, when there is acknowledgement of factors that impact its efficacy, and which present across the system, a sector, a phase and individual schools. Sustainable school and system improvement happens when there is a clear, agreed, shared and possibly emotive focus, a collective and deeply held desire, urgency and accountability to do better every day for everyone. It begins when we have the capacity and the desire to listen, to hear, to reflect and to change. It begins again every day with application of collective, intentional focus. It is the work of the whole system, to know, talk about and own what we aim to achieve together, and to own and prioritise focus, time and energy accordingly, as one.

 Further reading

Brown, B (2018) *Dare to Lead*. London: Vermilion.

Hargreaves, A and Shirley, D (2024) *The Age of Identity*. London: Sage.

Kotter, J P (2012) *Leading Change*. Boston: Harvard Business School Press.

Porritt, V and Featherstone, K (2019) *10% Braver: Inspiring Women to Lead Education*. London: Sage.

 References

Bunscoil Phobal Feirste (2024) School History. [online] Available at www.bunscoilphobalfeirste.com/page/School-History/369/Index. html#:~:text=In%20the%20late%2060%27s%20a,for%20the%20first%20 thirteen%20years (accessed 26 July 2024).

Comhairle na Gaelscolaíochta (2020) *IME Sector Development Plan (Draft)*. Belfast: Comhairle English.

Council for Curriculum, Examinations & Assessment (2009) *The Northern Ireland Curriculum (Gaelscolaíocht)*. [online] Available at https://ccea.org.uk/learning-resources/curaclam-thuaisceart-eireann-bunscolaiocht-gaelscolaiocht (accessed 6 May 2024).

Covey, S R (1989) *The 7 Habits of Highly Effective People*. London: Simon & Schuster.

The Northern Ireland Office (1998) *The Good Friday Agreement/The Belfast Agreement*. [online] Available at www.gov.uk/government/publications/the-belfast-agreement (accessed 6 May 2024).

6 Understanding the importance of cultural context and its place in supporting curriculum reform and pedagogy

KEVAN NAUGHTON

Key learning

- It is important to understand the global context and emphasis placed on curriculum reform within the Global Educational Reform Movement.

- We need to consider a profile of systemic 'pillars' required to support and underpin curriculum reform and teaching.

- It is necessary to understand the importance of mapping curriculum delivery, change and expectations alongside the best instructional pedagogies.

AoEA criteria

- Criterion 6: Working in concert with the school's leadership

- Criterion 8: Understanding the causal factors impacting on school performance

- Criterion 9: Providing critical evaluation of the quality of performance

- Criterion 10: Providing critical evaluation of the quality of leadership

- Criterion 11: Providing critical evaluation of the quality of teaching

- Criterion 14: Having up-to-date knowledge of relevant educational policy and other related issues

Introduction

What are the principles of curriculum reform? It is important to understand the *why*, *where* and *how*:

> *Curriculum is a structural series of intended learning outcomes. Curriculum prescribes (or at least anticipates) the results of instruction. It does not prescribe the means to be used in achieving the results.*
>
> (Johnson, 1967, p 128)

Raising curriculum expectations has long been seen as a key 'lever' to improve educational standards. PISA result comparisons and rankings have become an extension of governmental national pride.

Consequently, national curricula appear almost in a constant state of revision and exemplification. In the West, the United States, England, Sweden and Australia have all followed policies using standardised testing and a highly prescriptive curriculum, often at great expense. Such national and state curriculum models are referred to by Sahlberg (2015) as broadly following the Global Education Reform Movement (GERM) – a term that is used to heavily criticise this approach.

The merits of raising the curriculum expectation without providing support in reaching new goals and expectations are highly dubious and leave schools without capacity and vulnerable to falling behind. But just how do schools build systems that can adapt quickly to changes and increased expectations? To understand this, it might be better to begin by looking at the different tiers of curriculum change and what lies within the school's control.

Schools can do very little in response to changes at an international or even national level. Akka (2010) illustrates how international and comparative influences and 'supra-global trends' can be driven by external factors such as PISA results comparisons and ranking, which have become a source of governmental, national pride and a means by which to rank countries.

These and other trends may well lead schools to consider the interpretation of what 'meso', 'micro' and 'nano' (see Figures 6.1 and 6.2) changes may be required.

As a headteacher and National Leader of Education, advising schools on their personal curriculum journey involves various tiers of complexity. I believe understanding the contextual journey of each school can be very different and gathering a view of the uniqueness of each school is essential. Some key questions remain:

- Does the school have a strong 'platform' to manage curriculum reform in terms of evaluative leaders, systems and processes?

- Does the school know what the raised expectations will look and feel like at the deeply practical and bespoke level?

- Does the current level of pedagogical expertise ensure that opportunities can be planned and executed within lessons and teaching sequences?

To further develop my understanding of curriculum reform, I undertook research as part of a doctorate in educational leadership (DEL), which involved examining how schools have remained robust in their ability to adapt to change.

I began to appreciate that a series of 'pillars' underpin successful curriculum reform and once these pillars are successfully established, two broad 'reform pathways' emerge.

Understanding the systems that may need to be embedded to support effective curriculum reform

It is useful, as an adviser, to ascertain the systems that school leaders seek to build. These can be described as:

- accountability and quality assurance systems;

- stakeholder consultation and ensuring the curriculum matches expectations;

- leadership structures that support effective curriculum implementation involving coaching and mentoring support;
- collaborative support networks.

Figure 6.1 sets out a simple view of each system in terms of accountability, pastoral support, leadership and collaborative structures. These are not presented in a hierarchical way but are useful to interrogate in relation to the question of how any planned reform will be supported.

Through my own research, I have identified a second stage of analysis where I explored the weight and importance given to two specific strands of improvement or pathways that meet, intersect and interplay but need nourishment and support.

Pathway 1: Instructional teaching

The internal 'efficacy': to deliver, map, exemplify and clarify what must be taught based on:

- age to age;
- subject to subject;
- concept to concept.

Essentially, the teaching staff are coached in instructional techniques to specifically support high-quality teaching. Internal consistency requires time and systems to effectively monitor and quality assure this development. Schools that acknowledge a lack of internal capacity but go on to future success normally find creative ways to gain support in curriculum and are robust in their teaching development.

Considering which partnerships can directly influence their current or future capacity is key. As many studies have shown, those schools that are led best have a high focus on ongoing nurturing and development of instructional teaching (Fullan, 2003; Hopkins, 2007); in turn, these are best suited to reform and most adaptable to change.

Using a reform model supports true curriculum reform and deeper cultural change			
School and institution: Meso-school interpretation changes required *Classroom*: Micro-enactment of changes *Individual:* Nano-supporting access to curriculum			
Accountability structures: Quality assurance Evaluation and monitoring Appraisal	*Pastoral structures:* Behaviour management Role of contextual data Appointment to staffing structures Stakeholder trust and support	*Leadership structures:* Coaching Mentoring Measuring	*Collaborative structures:* Leadership peer support Identifying leaders Developing leaders
Indicators of having strong values: • Open, honest and reflective • Supportive and accepting • Make decisions with pupils at the centre • Appreciate the value of professional development *Values and practices to cause concern:* • Lack of internal consistent approaches • Weak interplay between the variety of stakeholders • Insufficient co-operation between the various roles within establishments at all levels			

Figure 6.1: Developing an understanding of what systems are already in place to support development and reform (Akker, 2010)

Seeing reform as both structural curriculum reform and as adhering to the principles of high-level instructional teaching, coaching and support allows schools to create teachers who are best suited to adapt and personalise both content and teaching techniques to support all pupils. Where this is done well, schools have a wide repertoire of instructional models and teaching techniques that are employed across the teaching sequence, to suit both content and inclusion.

A key question is whether there is a commitment to coached support. Have all considerations for each phase of school and each level of experience been considered?

Pathway 2: Curriculum design

The focus for reform ensures key non-negotiable elements that combine effectively in curriculum mapping and design. Do schools have a deeper understanding of what curriculum design looks like, such as:

- a high level of prescriptive content that builds foundational knowledge and 'a less is more' philosophy;
- named, trained and empowered leads who support implementation and understand the need to maintain;
- on-site ongoing training and regular exercises in standardisation and moderation;
- regular wider collaborative support, especially in the first year of implementation, and maintenance models thereafter;
- an understanding of how essential concepts can be stripped back and broken down into smaller steps to support greater inclusion;
- exemplification of standards – developing a 'nose for quality' and ensuring indicators of successful learning are in place and used as tools to assess accurately;
- the school having considered how information about progress is mapped, checked and quality assured;
- clearly established milestones to map and track.

Consider the strength of curriculum plans and, in a practical sense, how well the goals of the curriculum are understood by all. Do plans stand up to the scrutiny of the bullet points above? Figure 6.2 offers an articulation of this approach.

In summary, these aspects should be viewed as indicators of schools that have considered reforms alongside a 'system-focused' model.

Pillars

In terms of the contextual specifics of the school, how well developed is the school down the pathway of demonstrating clarity in its:

- accountability and quality assurance systems;
- stakeholder consultation;
- leadership structures and specific curriculum design developmental support;
- collaborative support networks?

Pathway 1

Is collective efficacy a non-negotiable for the school? Is there a range of professional development opportunities that support *how* the learning will be delivered:

- a commitment to system wide efficacy;
- instructional teaching pedagogical practice;
- coached support reflecting on teaching;
- a subject sequence-specific repertoire of teaching 'tools', such as how learning is summarised and recapped for pupils;
- personalisation and adaptation so adaptive teaching is turned to without a loss of pace?

Pathway 1	Pathway 2
Improvement through building the base of teacher efficacy	**Improvement via curriculum design, structure and exemplification**
Meso	*Meso*
Knowing the 'base' skills of staff	Clarifying the expectation
Supporting and developing the 'base'	Adapting the expectation in a mid- and long-term timeframe
Coaching and mentoring the 'base' with subject- and concept-specific pedagogical responses	Personalising the curriculum to meso specificity by:
	• key stage
Understanding effective assessment for learning (AFL) see below for an example of how this structure looks in detail	• cohort
	• phase specificity
	Building and exemplifying the expectation
Nano	*Nano*
Individualising coached practice and support for teachers. Teaching technique alongside subject specificity	Structures supporting inclusion through effectively knowing essential, limiting curriculum elements
Inclusion through personalisation of a range of teaching strategies (repertoire)	Inclusion via effective structuring of adaptation and intervention
Developing ubiquitous skills for effective inclusive teaching efficacy	Developing and resourcing effective catch-up programmes that run alongside teaching – within the curriculum design
Appraisal-based honest dialogue	Tracking and assessing the impact of the prescribed graduated response

Figure 6.2: A system-focused improvement strategy

Pathway 2

Have schools considered the essential learning that needs to take place within the *when* and the *where* of the teaching sequence:

- the removal of bureaucracy and creating shared unequivocal understanding of what is expected;
- contextualising the starting points of pupils;
- time taken to support and embed subject knowledge;
- an ongoing basic recovery programme for cohort, group and individuals, which is narrowing the attainment gap, over many months and even years;
- clarity of expectations of each year and the building blocks that interplay to build to this expected point;
- know that some essential elements need time to embed for some of their pupils (spiral design, catch up and keep up)?

Conclusion

Curriculum reform has become an inevitable factor of modern education. While it lies at the heart of our core business, clearly some schools are better placed than others to respond. The schools that give time and thought to operational models ensure the 'day to day' does not impact on their ability to plan strategically. The context of each school is unique, and ultimately will affect its ability to adapt and capacity to respond to change.

Supporting schools to consider the operational 'pillars' that support the system is a helpful starting point. Successful schools adapt and refine because they do not neglect their teaching 'base'; they support teachers to build a strong repertoire of teaching techniques that give teachers the essential ability to adapt to the needs of their children, both in lessons and across the teaching sequence.

Finally, if schools have considered what essential learning must be taught and learnt well, they have the ability to ensure strong starts are consistently built upon.

Some pupils will also need access to 'running repair' systems that ensure missed/partly conceived learning is covered and does not become a limiting factor in future learning.

 References

Akker, J (2010) *Beyond Lisbon 2010: Perspectives from Research and Development for Education Policy in Europe.* Dublin: Consortium of Institutions for Development and Research in Education in Europe.

Fullan, M (2003) *The Moral Imperative of School Leadership.* Thousand Oaks, CA: Corwin Press.

Hopkins, D (2007) *Every School a Great School.* Maidenhead: Open University Press.

Johnson, M (1967) Definitions and Models in Curriculum Theory. *Educational Theory*, 17(2): 127–40.

Sahlberg, P (2015) *Finnish Lessons 2.0* (2nd ed). New York: Teachers College Press.

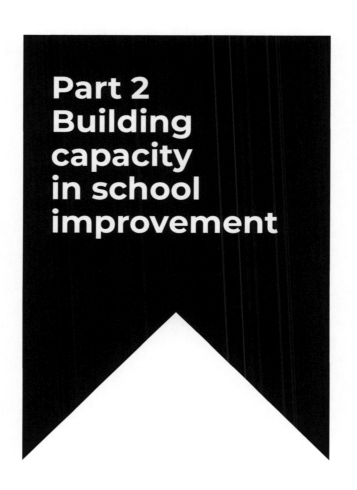

Part 2
Building
capacity
in school
improvement

7 'Unleashing greatness': the role of the school improvement adviser in building capacity

PROFESSOR DAVID HOPKINS

Key learning

- The adviser has a key role to play in helping to ensure that schools provide powerful and meaningful learning experiences for their children and young people, and that these positively impact on outcomes.

- Research evidence suggests that advisory support is far more effective when a proven strategy is utilised to focus development activity and energy. 'Unleashing greatness' offers the key components of such a strategy.

- A compelling and well-articulated moral purpose needs to inspire and be supported by a clarity of focus at the classroom level and a way of working with each other that enables leaders and teachers to learn from each other's best and that of others.

- In formulating school priorities, 'less means more'. Leaders' and teachers' energies should be focused on where impact will be greatest for all groups of learners – that is, in improving the quality of classroom practice.

AoEA criteria

- Criterion 6: Working in concert with the school's leadership

- Criterion 8: Understanding of causal factors impacting on school performance

- Criterion 10: Providing critical evaluation of the quality of leadership

- Criterion 11: Providing critical evaluation of the quality of teaching

- Criterion 13: Providing critical evaluation of collaborative working between governors, leaders and staff

- Criterion 14: Having an up-to-date knowledge of relevant educational policy, inspection and other related issues

Introduction

The adviser potentially plays a pivotal role in supporting school improvement. Indeed, the adviser's role is crucial in any systemic and strategic approach to educational development. In this chapter, the adviser's role in building middle-tier capacity is briefly reviewed before the 'Unleashing Greatness' school improvement framework is described. The 'Unleashing Greatness' framework provides advisers with a proven strategic approach for ensuring that their schools consistently create powerful learning experiences for students that result in enhanced academic success (Hopkins, 2024).

The adviser's role and middle-tier capacity

There is currently a myth of autonomy pervading school reform that is reflected in the increasing prevalence of 'right of centre' governments to embrace the trend towards the devolution of school management (Hopkins, 2013). The rhetoric is that if we let schools be free – release them from bureaucratic control and encourage independence – then they will flourish. This is a pervasive and populist image.

However, we know from the evidence of PISA (Mourshed et al, 2010; Schleicher, 2018) that there is no correlation between decentralisation and achievement, and that the world's best-performing educational systems sustain improvement by:

- establishing collaborative practices around teaching and learning;

- developing a mediating layer between the schools and the centre; and

- nurturing tomorrow's leadership.

The mediating layer role is one the adviser can play irrespective of the particular form of middle-tier architecture a system may have devised. To briefly summarise the evidence and analysis of Mourshed et al (2010, pp 23–24), advisers can help support school leaders; they often play a crucial role in identifying principals' development needs, managing school networks and lateral learning; they usually help identify and develop leadership capacity; and they help to strengthen and moderate accountability.

This chapter focuses specifically on the adviser role in supporting school improvement. In doing this, the evidence also suggests that such support is far more effective when a proven strategy is utilised to focus development activity and energy. In this case, it is the 'Unleashing Greatness' school improvement framework that is proposed (Hopkins, 2024).

The Unleashing Greatness framework

Although the eight steps of the 'Unleashing Greatness' framework are described sequentially, they are essentially interactive. The eight steps are just a starting point; however, they do provide a guide to action and summarise many of the key ideas in school improvement research, policy and practice. They also provide a guide for advisers in supporting their schools, and the questions at the end of each section act as a stimulus for reflection and a means of staying on track. The whole approach is described in far more detail in *Unleashing Greatness* (Hopkins 2024).

The eight steps are described below (see also Figure 7.1).

1. *Clarify moral purpose.* Ensure that the achievement and learning of students expressed as moral purpose is at the centre of everything that the school and teachers do.

2. *Focus on classroom practice.* The quality of a school or system cannot exceed the quality of its teachers: it is therefore axiomatic that the focus of school improvement is on the practice of teaching.

3. *Decide on the non-negotiables.* These are the key improvement objectives on which the school focuses unrelentingly in the short and medium term; they are underpinned by a 'development'

(as compared with a 'maintenance') structure that ensures adequate resources are made available for improvement work.

4. *Articulate the narrative*. Moral purpose may be at the heart of successful school and system improvement, but we will not realise this purpose without powerful and increasingly specified strategies and protocols embraced in a narrative that both energises and provides direction for our colleagues, students and communities.

5. *Utilise instructional rounds and theories of action*. These are the key strategies for diagnosing and articulating effective teaching practice through non-judgemental observation and the development of protocols to ensure consistency and precision.

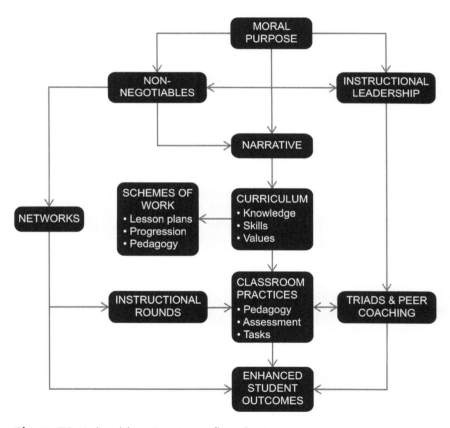

Figure 7.1: Unleashing Greatness flowchart

6. *Embrace peer coaching and triads.* Provide the infrastructure for professional development in the school and the means for putting the theories of action into practice.

7. *Practise instructional leadership.* Is the leadership strategy most closely associated with increased levels of student achievement through the employment of four key behaviours: setting vision; managing teaching and learning; developing people and organisation redesign?

8. *Exploit networking.* The most effective schools network with each other to learn from their best, collaborate purposefully and share outstanding practice.

Clarify moral purpose

Moral purpose is not to be confused or equated with some form of romantic sentimentalism. It is clear from the global evidence of school performance that the most successful schools ensure that the achievement and learning of students expressed as moral purpose is at the centre of all that teachers and leaders do. Aspirations such as 'enabling every student to realise their potential' are fine as far as it goes, but we then have to define in more concrete and contextual terms what that means for our students. This requires a focus on those strategies that have a track record of accelerating student achievement, such as building student learning capability, personalising learning and the curriculum, assessment for learning and giving students a voice in their own learning.

Moral purpose may be at the heart of successful school and system improvement, yet schools will not be able to realise this purpose without powerful and specified strategies and tools to allow them to deal with the increasingly turbulent and complex communities and contexts they serve. The key is that moral purpose and strategic action are opposite sides of the same coin.

Key questions

- Does the school's version of moral purpose link aspiration to action?

- Does the school's version of moral purpose reflect the values of students, parents and the community?

- Is the school's version of moral purpose widely accepted by the whole school staff?

Focus on classroom practice

Barber and Mourshed's (2007, p 40) widely referenced international study based on the PISA research concludes that:

- the quality of an education system cannot exceed the quality of its teachers;

- the only way to improve outcomes is to improve instruction;

- this means taking professional development into the classroom and making it routine – for example, through peer observation, lesson study, demonstration lessons.

We need to reach down into the classroom and deepen reform efforts by moving beyond superficial curriculum change to a more profound understanding of how teacher behaviour connects to learning. In particular, it requires a direct and unrelenting focus on what many are now calling the 'instructional core'. This is composed of the teacher and the student in the presence of content (City et al, 2009). There are four components to this: curriculum; teaching strategies; learning skills; and assessment for learning.

Two features require emphasising from the outset.

1. One element of the instructional core cannot be changed without impacting directly on the others.

2. There is an appreciation that the 'instructional task' is at the centre of the instructional core. The instructional task is the actual work that students do as part of classroom practice. It is this that predicts their performance, especially when the task is firmly located within the student's 'zone of proximal development'.

Key questions

- Do the school staff understand the importance of the instructional core, both strategically and operationally?

- Are all the tasks that students undertake located within their zones of proximal development?

- Are the teaching practices employed in the school well specified, consistently applied and directly applicable to the learning needs of all students?

Decide on the non-negotiables

Many schools are overloaded by pressure for change and policy initiatives. With the best of intentions, they try to do everything and end up doing nothing well. Michael Fullan advised our schools some years ago to just do one or two things as well as they possibly could, then do everything else as well as they would have done anyway. These non-negotiables become the key development objectives on which the school focuses unrelentingly in the short and medium term. They are underpinned by a 'development' (compared with a 'maintenance') structure that ensures that adequate resources are made available for improvement work, in particular the identification of a school improvement team and peer coaching.

The *maintenance structure* is concerned with relatively permanent systems and processes that are necessary for the school to get its work done as efficiently as possible. The *development structure* is there to adopt new ways of working – the non-negotiables – that, over time, add value to the school as new practices become common practice and turn into the 'way we do things around here'. The three key elements of the school's development structure are the establishment of a school improvement team, peer coaching and teacher collaboration.

Key questions

- Is the whole staff clear about what the non-negotiables are in the school and whether they are actively working on them?

- Is there a distinction between the maintenance and development functions in the school, particularly the purposes, funding and responsibilities involved?

- Is there a school improvement team in the school and how does it operate?

Articulate the narrative

Stories help us make sense of where we are and remember where we are headed. Moral purpose may be at the heart of successful school and system improvement, but we will not realise this purpose without powerful and increasingly specified strategies and protocols embraced in a narrative to take the school forward. This both energises and provides direction for our colleagues, students and communities.

Good school improvement stories have the following characteristics. They:

- are *urgent* – they translate the vision of curiosity, of a focus on inquiry, into clear principles for action;

- offer a *motivating* image of the future we are creating for our school and our students;

- link *moral purpose* to action in practical and concrete ways – our values are the constant companions of our actions;

- make *tangible connections* between teaching and learning. These connections sustain a teaching and learning culture that produces and maintains high standards and student empowerment;

- are *inclusive* and *oriented to action* in every classroom and across the whole school;

- are *shared and understood* by staff, students and the school community.

A story is a flight simulator for the mind: we can chart a new direction and vividly see where it takes us. It is this vividness that schools and system leaders can summon through stories. It is a vividness about both seeing the path ahead and taking that path – it is about acting with clarity.

Key questions

- Does the school's narrative link moral purpose to action?

- Does the core story describe the direction in which the school is moving and what success will look like – the desired state?

- Is the narrative understood and owned by all sections of the school community – students, staff, parents and governors?

Instructional rounds and theories of action

We use the *instructional rounds* process that utilises non-judgemental (appreciative) observation to develop a shared understanding and common language around effective teaching practices; to recognise what good teaching and good student learning looks like; and to identify the next level of work for the school and network. The outcome of the process is the identification of a set of *theories of action* for the school and network that can be used as a basis for further professional development and school improvement. The *theories of action* provide the basis of the protocols we have developed that ensure precision, consistency and engagement in the classrooms of our schools (Hopkins et al, 2018).

Through our experience with instructional rounds, we have learned that, despite the phase or context of schooling, the *theories of action* generated by each school were in most cases very similar:

- harnessing learning intentions, narrative and pace;

- setting challenging learning tasks;

- framing higher order questions;

- scaffolding student learning;

- committing to assessment for learning;

- implementing co-operative group structures.

It is important to note that all these *theories of action* are characterised by an approach to teaching that has inquiry and personalised learning at its centre. They also have a high level of empirical support (see Hattie, 2009) and are consistent with most policy and accountability prescriptions related to effective teaching.

Key questions

- Does the school staff regularly engage in *instructional rounds* and appreciate that the focus of the observations is on description, not evaluation or judgement?

- How far do the six theories of action reflect common consistent and widespread practice in the school?

- Does the school's school improvement team contextualise and provide examples of the *theories of action* related to the specific context of teaching and learning in the school?

Peer coaching and triads

The strategy most suited to the acquisition of the *theories of action* is the now-established approach to the 'peer coaching' process developed by Bruce Joyce and his colleagues (Joyce and Calhoun, 2010). Their research on staff development has identified several key training components:

1. presentation of theory or description of skill or strategy;

2. modelling or demonstration of skills or models of teaching;

3. practice in simulated and classroom settings;

4. structured and open-ended feedback (provision of information about performance);

5. *peer coaching* for application (hands-on, in-classroom assistance with the transfer of skills and strategies to the classroom).

It is also helpful to identify where these various forms of staff development are best located – either in the 'workshop' or the 'workplace'. The workshop is where teachers gain understanding, see demonstrations of the teaching strategy they may wish to acquire and have an opportunity to practise them in a non-threatening environment. This constitutes Steps 1–4 above. If the aim, however, is to transfer those skills back into the workplace – the classroom and school – then merely attending the workshop is insufficient. What is required is the opportunity for immediate and sustained practice, collaboration and peer coaching within triads or small groups of staff – Step 5. Peer observation within triads needs to be scheduled on a regular basis and built into the timetable. This need not be time consuming: 15 to 20 minutes, observation when using the protocol is usually sufficient.

Key questions

- Does every member of staff belong to a peer coaching group?

- Do the peer coaching groups meet regularly as part of timetabled staff development activity?

- How far do the outcomes of these *peer observations* contribute to higher standards of learning and teaching in the school?

Instructional leadership

Instructional leadership is the leadership approach most closely associated with increased levels of student achievement (Leithwood, Harris and Hopkins, 2019). In this widely cited article, we describe the four central domains of instructional leadership as seen in Figure 7.2, and the seven strong claims of leadership behaviours. This analysis reinforces the argument that enhancing learning and teaching is the key priority for school leadership.

Setting direction	Ensuring that the school's vision sees every learner reach their potential.
	Translating this vision into a whole-school curriculum and high expectations.
Managing teaching and learning	Ensuring a high degree of consistency by planning, implementing and using specifications of practice.
	Supporting innovation in teaching practices that enable personalised learning for all students, by expanding the repertoire of teaching practice to include high leverage practices that influence the learning of all students.
Developing people	Enabling students to become active learners.
	Creating a school that operates as a professional learning community for teachers.
Developing the organisation	Creating an evidence-based school and an effective organisation.
	Participating in collaborative networks that build curriculum diversity, professional support and extended services.

Figure 7.2: The four central domains of instructional leadership

Key questions

- How far are the *seven strong claims* (Leithwood, Harris and Hopkins, 2019) evident in the leadership behaviours in the school?

- What proportion of their working time are the senior leaders in the school focusing on the four key behaviours? If it is not 75 per cent or above, why not?

- Is there a development or implementation plan in the school that leads coherently and strategically in identifiable phases from narrative to eventual culture change?

Networking

If a school's improvement journey is to be sustained over the long term, support has to be integrated into the very fabric of the system pedagogy. The most effective networks have assumed this role and developed productive ways of learning from their best, for collaborating purposefully and sharing outstanding practice (Hopkins, 2022).

In England at the present time, the most common middle-tier organisation is the Multi-Academy Trust (MAT) (Hopkins, 2016). In outstanding MATs, capacity is built at the local level to ensure that all those in the trust's family of schools progress as rapidly as possible towards excellence.

In moving to scale, several things are clear from international benchmarking studies of school performance (Hopkins, 2013):

- There is a need for professional support within the system to connect the centre to schools and schools to each other – *advisers linked to academy chains and MATs can provide this function.*

- Investment in head/principal and leadership training is essential – *hence the use of frameworks such as these eight steps to guide action.*

- The quality of teaching is the best determinant of student performance – *thus the focus in high-performing trusts on the progress of learners and the development of teachers.*

- Outstanding educational systems find ways of learning from the best – *which is why capacity needs to be built not only within trusts but also between them at the system level.*

Key questions

- Is the school a member of an established network or MAT?

- If so, does the network or MAT have a coherent and systematic approach to capacity-building?

- In the network, is best practice shared and is every school on an improvement trajectory?

Coda: school improvement pathway

It is now well established that schools are at various stages or phases of development (Hopkins, 2013). So, although the phases or steps of this generic improvement model all need to be followed, they also have to be adapted to the context or stage of development of the individual school. Doing this is one of the essential skills of an adviser.

The *school improvement pathway* was developed to assist with this process of adaptation and contextualisation (Hopkins and Craig, 2018, pp 24–28). The school improvement pathway is a framework that assists advisers and school leaders to diagnose current orientations to student learning, and from that diagnosis to map a pathway to excellence. Each school begins its improvement journey at a different point on the school improvement pathway. The performance continuum describes schools as moving along a pathway from 'awful to adequate', 'adequate to good', 'good to great' and 'great to excellent'.

The adviser also needs to be alert to the combination of strategies needed to move a school along the continuum from 'awful to adequate' to 'great to excellent'. When systems and schools use this knowledge strategically, they make significant and rapid progress.

The pathway also specifies five improvement dimensions: curriculum; teaching; learning; assessment and accountability; and leadership. It identifies key issues that emerge along the school improvement continuum and poses a series of questions that advisers can use to help progress development.

What excellence means for each school evolves continually. We must adapt the school's narrative and improvement plans so they remain relevant to changing context. Ongoing adaptation is facilitated by regularly reassessing where the school is situated on the school improvement pathway. This is the real work of the school improvement adviser in assisting schools to unleash greatness.

References

Barber, M and Mourshed, M (2007) *How the World's Best Performing School Systems Come Out on Top*. London: McKinsey & Company.

City, E A, Elmore, R F, Fiarman, S E and Teitel, L (2009) *Instructional Rounds in Education: A Network Approach to Improving Teaching and Learning*. Cambridge, MA: Harvard University Press.

Hattie, J (2009) *Visible Learning: A Synthesis of Over 800 Meta-analyses Relating to Achievement*. London: Routledge.

Hopkins, D (2013) *Exploding the Myths of School Reform*. Maidenhead: Open University Press.

Hopkins, D (2016) Building Capacity for School Improvement in Multi-academy Trusts – From the Inside Out. *SSAT Journal,* 7: 19–29.

Hopkins, D (2022) The Role of Networks in Supporting School Improvement. In Handscomb, G and Brown, C (eds), *The Power of Professional Learning Networks*. Woodbridge: John Catt Educational. Available at: www.profdavidhopkins.com/assets/docs/Role%20of%20Networks%20_1.pdf (accessed 29 June 2024).

Hopkins, D (2024) *Unleashing Greatness: A Strategy for School Improvement*. Woodbridge: John Catt Educational.

Hopkins, D and Craig, W (2018) *Leadership for Powerful Learning*. Sydney: Pearson Education.

Hopkins, D, Craig, W and Knight O (2018) *Curiosity and Powerful Learning*. Sydney: Pearson Education.

Joyce, B and Calhoun, E (2010), *Models of Professional Development*. Thousand Oaks, CA: Corwin Press.

Leithwood, K, Harris, A and Hopkins, D (2019) Seven Strong Claims About Successful School Leadership Revisited. *School Leadership & Management*, 40(1): 5–22.

Mourshed, M, Chijioke, C and Barber, M (2010) *How the World's Most Improved School Systems Keep Getting Better*, London: McKinsey and Company.

Schleicher, A (2018) *World Class: How to Build a 21st Century School System*. Paris: OECD.

8 The role of the education adviser in enabling middle leaders to improve performance

EMMA TARRANT

Key learning

- A number of common challenges can limit the effectiveness of middle leaders, despite their importance to embedding effective practice in the classroom. They include role ambiguity, workload pressures, a lack of appropriate experience and training. Advisers can provide support in overcoming such barriers to professional impact.

- Middle leaders benefit from ongoing support and professional development to enhance their leadership skills and effectiveness in driving school improvement. Access to relevant training opportunities and mentoring from external advisers can help address skill gaps and build capacity to impact.

- Modelling and coaching are powerful strategies for supporting the development of middle leaders in schools. Conducting a thorough needs assessment to identify the specific areas where middle leaders require coaching and mentoring support is vital. This may include assessing leadership skills, pedagogical knowledge, strategic planning abilities and interpersonal communication skills.

- Advisers face challenges such as time constraints, assessing impact and facing resistance to their authority. By prioritising tasks, assessing impact through reflective discussions and building trust and credibility through collaboration and evidence-based practices, advisers can navigate these challenges effectively.

AoEA criteria

- Criterion 6: Working in concert with the school's leadership

- Criterion 8: Understanding of causal factors impacting on school performance

- Criterion 14: Having an up-to-date knowledge of relevant educational policy and other related issues

Introduction

Middle leaders are uniquely placed to act as a bridge between senior leaders and the classroom, providing a perspective that is deeply rooted in the practicalities of everyday school life. As educational advisers, we must recognise the role they play in implementing change at a tangible level. Advisers are uniquely placed to support, challenge and empower middle leaders to drive improvement, innovation and excellence in teaching and learning within their respective departments.

In this chapter I will share how, in my 15 years as an education adviser, I have worked in a variety of maintained schools and academies. I begin by outlining some of the challenges faced by middle leaders. Next, I will explore how I have engaged middle leaders through understanding who they are and the context in which they work, using a model I have found particularly effective. Supporting middle leaders to develop strategic awareness is vital to their impact and growth into future senior leaders, if they aspire to that. Lastly, I will explain the vital importance of professional learning for middle leaders and how advisers can support this.

Challenges for middle leaders

Despite their critical role in driving school improvement, middle leaders can encounter various challenges that limit their effectiveness. For this reason, it is crucial to take time to understand the context in which a middle leader is working so we are best placed to tailor our support and development opportunities to meet individual needs. Below are examples of common challenges faced by middle leaders.

Role ambiguity

Middle leaders such as department heads, team leaders or subject leads can face role ambiguity for a range of reasons:

- lack of a clear job description or role profile;
- overlapping responsibilities;
- limited authority;
- changing organisational priorities.

When working with a middle leader, I suggest an initial conversation to establish the extent to which they have a clear, comprehensive job description outlining their roles, responsibilities and expectations, as ambiguity can lead to uncertainty about what tasks they should prioritise and how they should allocate their time. There are also occasions when these expectations are clear but middle leaders are less confident in their understanding and value the chance to explore them with an external adviser.

Clarity is important where responsibilities overlap with those of other leaders or administrators within the school. This will avoid confusion about who is accountable for specific tasks or decisions.

Where middle leaders have limited delegated decision-making power or autonomy, it can be challenging for them to effectively fulfil their roles. It is essential that we help to clarify the extent of their influence and boundaries of their responsibilities within the leadership structure.

I also seek to understand organisational dynamics and how middle leaders can more effectively be involved to support their understanding of strategic direction. When changes in priorities, policies or initiatives are not clearly communicated by senior leaders, or are implemented inconsistently, middle leaders may struggle to understand or adapt to their evolving responsibilities.

Workload pressures

Middle leaders have significant teaching responsibilities, so their effective use of time is paramount to their success. In my experience, there are two issues: role overload and an unclear reporting structure. A significant number of middle leaders are juggling teaching responsibilities alongside leadership. This can result in limited time for leadership and an excessive workload, with multiple tasks and responsibilities competing for attention. When overwhelmed, these middle leaders may struggle to prioritise effectively.

If it is unclear exactly to whom they should report, or where they should seek guidance or escalate issues, middle leaders often hold on to problems and responsibilities that could easily be delegated. Seeking clarity around organisational reporting and accountability is essential.

Lack of role-matched training and support

The effectiveness of middle leaders can be compromised by a lack of appropriate and timely professional development. This can be particularly apparent in three areas: pedagogical knowledge; leadership; and resistance to change.

Middle leaders play a crucial role in shaping the instructional practices within their departments or teams. Middle leaders lacking pedagogical knowledge in specific areas will struggle to provide meaningful guidance and support to teachers in their departments or teams. The early promotion of relatively experienced teachers into middle leader roles, sometimes reflecting their potential and sometimes to aid recruitment and retention, can present a challenge. Despite their enthusiasm, energy and subject knowledge, they may not have mastered their grasp of pedagogical knowledge. This also happens when middle leaders change roles or schools, and encounter new challenges in curriculum or meeting pupil needs. This lack of pedagogical knowledge can result in a lack of direction and coherence, have a poor impact on the quality of teaching and ultimately weaken outcomes.

Middle leaders may not receive sufficient training or support to help them understand their roles and responsibilities fully. Within secondary settings, middle leaders may directly line-manage a deputy and performance-manage at least half a department team. Without adequate preparation or ongoing professional development, they may feel uncertain about how to effectively lead their teams or departments. In primary settings, many middle leaders are expected to matrix manage across the whole school despite having no line management responsibilities or authority.

When implementing change and introducing new practices, middle leaders may encounter resistance. They must know how to navigate resistance effectively, engaging stakeholders in the change process and fostering a shared vision for improvement. Education advisers are able to offer perspective and experience to support middle leaders navigate these challenges, offering an understanding of change-management principles.

Improving middle leaders' impact

Middle leaders benefit from ongoing support and professional development to enhance their leadership skills and effectiveness in driving school improvement. Access to relevant training opportunities and mentoring can help address skill gaps and build capacity among middle leaders.

Modelling and coaching are powerful strategies for supporting the development of middle leaders in schools. By witnessing effective leadership behaviours at first hand, middle leaders can gain insights into best practices and develop a clearer understanding of how to apply them in their own contexts.

Conducting a thorough needs assessment to identify the specific areas where middle leaders require coaching and mentoring support is vital. This may include assessing leadership skills, pedagogical knowledge, strategic planning abilities and interpersonal communication skills.

Example 1: From managing to leading

I regularly refer to the Steve Radcliffe FED model of leadership – future, engage and deliver. This model provides a practical framework for middle leaders to focus on key leadership areas such as vision-setting, relationship-building, execution and accountability, ultimately helping them to fulfil their roles more effectively.

Future

- *Vision setting.* Middle leaders need to develop a compelling vision for their area of responsibility within the school. I begin by exploring this area in some detail and, through careful questioning and guidance, support them to articulate a clear picture of what their vision is and how it aligns with the school's strategic direction.

- *Strategic planning.* Middle leaders need to engage in strategic planning processes to identify priorities, opportunities and challenges within their area. I do this through reverse engineering – supporting them to clarify their end goal in terms of changes to leadership, teacher and pupil behaviours, identify what success looks like in each of these layers and which specific actions are required to ensure their individual efforts or efforts of a team contribute to the school's broader goals.

Engage

- *Building relationships.* When middle leaders focus on building relationships with their team members, colleagues, students, parents and other stakeholders, they can create a positive and inclusive team culture where individuals feel valued, heard and motivated to contribute. I take time to identify how messages will be communicated to colleagues around the goals, benefits and expected outcomes of any proposed change. I also support middle leaders in identifying opportunities for collective contribution as this not only boosts morale, but also leads to more effective implementation.

Deliver

- *Execution and accountability.* Middle leaders can focus on delivering results by effectively executing plans, managing resources and holding themselves and their team members accountable for outcomes. I support middle leaders to set clear expectations, monitor progress and adjust strategies as needed to achieve desired goals.

- *Problem-solving and decision-making.* Middle leaders can develop their ability to solve problems and make decisions in a timely and effective manner. They may need support in the use of data, evidence and input from stakeholders to inform their decision-making process and address challenges proactively.

By applying the FED model, I have successfully coached middle leaders to enhance their leadership effectiveness, inspire their teams and drive positive change within their schools.

Example 2: Strategic planning

In my experience, a significant focus of the educational adviser's work with middle leaders is the development of strategic planning and the implementation cycle. It is necessary to ensure that middle leaders understand implementation is a process, not an event, and that they plan and execute it in stages:

> *Successful implementation happens in stages and unfolds over an extended period of time. It is not a single event that takes place when the decision to adopt a new teaching practice is made, or on the day when training begins. Schools' implementation processes begin before this adoption decision and last for a long time after.*
>
> (EEF, 2021)

Identification of priorities and key actions to address these

The adviser may need to conduct an initial assessment with the middle leader to understand the current challenges, goals and areas for improvement within the school setting. This assessment should help to identify priorities. Depending on the experience and skillset of the middle leader, support may be required to review data, evaluating progress of specific cohorts and groups of pupils for patterns and trends.

I always work collaboratively with the middle leader to identify potential solutions and establish clear, specific and achievable goals that align with the needs of the department or team. These goals can serve as the foundation for action planning.

Action planning

Having identified the goals, I then support the identification of the specific steps, timelines and resources needed to achieve these. The plan should be strategic, realistic and measurable. Guidance on how to effectively allocate resources, such as time, budget and personnel, to support the implementation of the action plan may need to be provided.

Monitoring

I help the middle leader establish mechanisms for monitoring progress towards their goals, such as regular check-ins, progress reports and data analysis. This ongoing monitoring ensures accountability and allows for adjustments to the action plan as needed.

Review and next steps

Regular opportunities to review progress against the agreed action plan are an essential part of this process. I always plan opportunities to return and evaluate progress against agreed milestones. This allows me to identify progress, offer strategies for overcoming obstacles and provide constructive feedback and support to the middle leader.

During these return visits, it is important to recognise and celebrate successes and milestones achieved by the middle leader. This positive reinforcement helps maintain motivation and momentum for continued growth and improvement.

Example 3: Professional learning

Education advisers can play a crucial role in supporting middle leaders in their professional learning and development.

Conduct a needs assessment to identify the specific learning needs and goals of middle leaders

This could involve surveys, interviews or focus groups to gather feedback from middle leaders about their professional development priorities and areas for growth. Advisers can then work with middle leaders to develop customised learning plans based on their findings. These plans could include a combination of bespoke workshops, courses, coaching sessions and self-directed learning activities. Access to a variety of resources, including research articles, books, courses, webinars and other professional development material, is essential.

Facilitate workshops and training sessions specifically designed for middle leaders

These workshops could cover topics such as leadership skills development, effective communication, strategic planning, team-building, data analysis and problem-solving.

Use coaching and mentoring support to help middle leaders develop their leadership skills, overcome challenges, and achieve their professional goals

By offering tailored support, access to resources, and opportunities for collaboration and reflection, education advisers can empower middle leaders to enhance their leadership effectiveness and drive positive change within their schools and communities.

Challenges for education advisers

As an experienced education adviser, I am very familiar with the challenges we can face in fulfilling our role effectively. Below, I have identified some of the common challenges and outlined how I address these when working with middle leaders.

Time constraints

The amount of time available to work directly within an education setting can vary considerably. It is therefore essential to prioritise tasks based on urgency and importance: identifying where quick fixes are required and where longer developmental programmes are necessary. Once priorities are established, I agree a schedule of visits and establish a detailed programme of support, clarifying expectations around intersessional tasks to free up more time for meaningful interactions. Where visits are infrequent, I always encourage middle leaders to stay connected between and set clear expectations for communication frequency. This allows me to provide ongoing guidance and remote feedback when required.

Assessing impact

Measuring the impact of advisory support can be challenging, especially when tangible outcomes are not immediately evident. I always start each visit with an opportunity to engage middle leaders in reflective discussions. This allows me to evaluate the effectiveness of key actions or interventions taken so far and support them to adjust strategies as needed.

Where little or no impact is evident, I complete a thorough assessment to identify the root causes of the limited impact. This may involve reviewing data, observing classroom practices and interviewing stakeholders to gain insights into the challenges faced by the middle leader. These findings are then used to further refine the programme of support and may lead to additional opportunities for coaching.

Challenges to authority

There are times when we all experience resistance or scepticism from others who question our expertise or authority. I have found that when working with middle leaders, trust and credibility are built through active listening, empathy and collaboration. I always respect the knowledge and experience of the people with whom I work, understand their unique strength and challenges, and tailor the support provided accordingly. It is also essential to base advice and recommendations on objective evidence and best practices. I therefore ensure that I remain well informed in current educational research and use data-driven decision-making to guide my advice and support.

Conclusion

Middle leaders serve as a crucial link between senior leadership and the classroom, but they face various challenges such as role ambiguity, workload pressures and a lack of training and support. It is vital for educational advisers to understand these challenges and tailor their support accordingly.

Education advisers can support middle leaders by providing tailored guidance, coaching and professional development opportunities. Strategies such as clarifying roles and responsibilities, facilitating strategic planning and fostering professional learning can help middle leaders to overcome obstacles and enhance their effectiveness.

Advisers themselves face challenges such as time constraints, assessing impact and facing resistance to their authority. By prioritising tasks, assessing impact through reflective discussions and building trust and credibility through collaboration and evidence-based practices, advisers can navigate these challenges effectively.

References

Education Endowment Fund (EEF) (2021) *Putting Evidence to Work: A School's Guide to Implementation.* Available at: https://educationendo wmentfoundation.org.uk (accessed 24 April 2024).

Radcliffe, S (2012) *Leadership Plain and Simple.* London: Pearson Education.

9 Successfully supporting the recruitment, retention and development of new teachers

MICHAELA BARBER

Key learning

- Education advisers can play an import role in ensuring that schools have the important capacities needed to support the recruitment and retention of early career teachers (ECTs).

- Advisers can provide further support by evaluating the extent to which the school is making effective provision for ECTs' development and help to address any emerging performance issues.

- Supporting an effective learning community for ECTs in the wider educational community builds professional resilience.

AoEA criteria

- Criterion 6: Working in concert with the school's leadership

- Criterion 14: Having an up-to-date knowledge of relevant educational policy and other related issues

Introduction

Throughout my career, I have been fortunate enough to be supported by a wide range of passionate and talented professionals who have inspired and influenced me to be the best teacher, and then headteacher, that I can be. I would argue that this should not be an arbitrary luck of the draw but instead a guaranteed pathway for all professionals throughout their career. However, these opportunities are most important for those who are new to the profession – novices learning their craft and therefore most in need of a nurturing structure that enables growth and confidence.

In England, there is an urgency to improve the recruitment and retention of early career teachers (ECTs). Overall, postgraduate teacher recruitment as measured Initial Teacher Training (ITT) census data has been consistently low in recent academic years and some 35–40% below recruitment targets. This is mainly driven by very low recruitment numbers for secondary trainee teachers. Initial primary recruitment is just below target.

The National Foundation for Education Research (NFER) has reported the implications of the current recruitment challenges:

> *National data on the teacher labour market suggests that the supply of new trainees is insufficient to meet future demand, which implies that schools are likely to face challenges recruiting teachers, perhaps leading to staff shortages.*
> (Worth and Faulkner-Ellis, 2022)

Retention is also a concern. For example, the Department for Education (DfE) schools workforce data 2021 reported that 12.5 per cent of teachers have left the profession after only one year, 23 per cent within three years and 31.2 per cent within five years (DfE, 2021).

In this chapter, I explore the value of appointing ECTs within schools and examine the role of education advisers in supporting the successful induction and retention of colleagues new to the profession. I offer some examples about what I have personally been involved in, as well as drawing on best practices that I have witnessed through my role as an education adviser, a member of an 'Appropriate Body' team, responsible for moderating and supporting ECTs and their schools, and as a facilitator in the delivery of the Early Career Framework (ECF).

Considering school capacity when considering whether to appoint an early career teacher

The capacity to successfully support ECTs comes in many shapes and sizes. There are several key features that need to be considered to ensure infrastructure is in place to provide an effective framework for those new to the profession. As an education adviser, the opportunity to influence the creation of a successful environment for ECTs naturally begins with discussions with school leaders, in supporting headteachers and senior leaders to understand the considerations that sit behind recruiting an ECT and that are paramount to a successful appointment. This is especially true when the school is new to appointing ECTs and maybe unaware of the support package that will be needed.

The best environments in which ECTs can thrive are evident when the school can appoint an experienced member of staff as an induction tutor. This should be an excellent practitioner who is skilled in making evaluative judgements against the Teachers' Standards. They should be confident in evaluating the extent to which the ECT is successfully progressing to achieve all teacher standards by the end of the second year.

Regular review meetings, tracking of professional development opportunities and feedback from lesson observations provide the vehicle for the induction tutor to be well informed to give purposeful feedback and identify next steps with the ECT. When less successful, induction tutor feedback is not precise and the ECT is unclear about the expectations and is likely to be overwhelmed by trying to work on all elements of the teaching standards at the same time. A key element of success is to provide the training and moderation for the induction tutor, particularly if the induction tutor is new to the role or is the only one in the school. This enables them to be secure in their judgements when using the teacher standards. As a result, both the induction tutor and the ECT will have a shared clarity of what is going well and the next steps to be focused upon. There is a shared understanding of expectations, and the support is then targeted to meet the identified needs.

A second consideration is the importance of a dedicated mentor, ideally separate from the induction tutor. This provides a structure of support to the ECT through their two-year continuous professional development programme. As an adviser, I have helped school leaders understand and value the difference between this role and that of the induction tutor. The key here is that the mentor has a focus on supporting the ECT to be a reflective and self-improving practitioner. I have found that there is an accelerated rate of development when the school provides protected time to ensure coaching from the mentor on any identified next step. The use of instructional coaching and deliberate practice helps the ECT to build their mental model as they move from novice to expert teacher over time.

Equipped with this knowledge, an education adviser helps leaders to evaluate their school's capacity to provide this important level of support. Where schools are already effective in their cycle of self-improvement and able to swiftly identify their improvement priorities, with structures in place to provide a continuous professional development pathway for all their staff, such capacity is often evident. Schools that have capacity to grow their staff already share and embed practice and leaders are mindful of the ways in which they will integrate the support for the ECT.

In contrast, the appointment of ECTs is less successful when school leaders and staff are focused primarily on day-to-day operational matters or lack the capacities identified above. This can be a particular challenge within underperforming schools and sometimes in very small schools. The appointment of an ECT where capacity is very limited will often be problematic for all concerned. Therefore, advisers may find it helpful to work with headteachers on a Strengths, Weaknesses, Opportunities and Threats (SWOT) analysis of the school's capacity before appointing an ECT.

Once it is established that the school has capacity, there are both advantages and disadvantages to appointing more than one ECT within a school or department. By default, the need for senior teacher support may double. However, the benefits of creating an environment of support can be strengthened as the ECTs can be encouraged to use their ECT time to learn from and reflect with one another.

Assuring the quality of early career teacher support and progress

Education advisers are ideally placed to take a lead role in evaluating the extent to which the school is making effective provision for the ECTs so they feel supported and able to make a positive contribution to the school community. An evaluative 360 review session is an effective way to gather the views of all personnel involved in the ECT induction process, with an opportunity to reflect back the findings, celebrate the strengths of the provision and suggest areas that could be further strengthened.

There are, of course, rare occasions when an ECT is not making the required progress and the school needs to address underperformance. The need to be open, honest and transparent while still demonstrating a desire to support is a balance that many headteachers find challenging. Again, the adviser can be part of a supportive process, using the Teacher Standards to specifically identify and address the areas requiring focus. Working with school leaders and ECTs, external advisers can help broker a support plan, with clear criteria and training to be provided within time expectations. My experience is that successful outcomes are more likely when the gaps in understanding or performance can be swiftly identified and opportunities found to address these without the ECT feeling that all is lost. In these situations, I have found that an external adviser used for lesson observation and feedback can provide everyone with an objective and helpful evaluation against the Teacher Standards.

When things are not going as well as expected, a complex mix of school and individual contributory factors is sometimes at play. The adviser's independence, objectivity and sensitivity to what is at stake can help to establish a positive way forward for everyone involved and head off a downward spiral in what can sometimes be a highly emotive situation.

Building a support network for early career teachers beyond the school

Another key role of the adviser, enriching the school's own support, can be to provide a forum for ECTs to develop a learning community where they can feel a sense of belonging and share experiences with those at a similar point in their professional life.

Lenning and Ebbers (1999) refer to four broad areas to be considered when building a successful learning community:

- a sense of belonging;
- interdependence or reliance among the members;
- trust among members;
- faith or trust in the shared purpose of the community.

Anecdotal feedback from ECTs is that they prefer to meet in a physical face-to-face environment with plenty of opportunities to talk and reflect with their peers. However, across a wider geographical area, this can also be organised effectively with online meetings that have opportunities for breakout room discussions. Either of these, or a combination of both, can be effective through the expert facilitation of an adviser or guest speaker in conferences and shorter ECT group sessions.

In my experience, the most powerful and supportive sessions, which build successful learning communities, happen when a clear agenda is shared in advance so ECTs have time to prepare their thoughts or questions. ECT feedback reports that sessions focused on direct instruction on best practice examples, coupled with practical ways to develop their understanding of classroom pedagogy and curriculum development, are the most beneficial. However, facilitators of these learning communities also need to be flexible and responsive to the requirements of the ECTs and give appropriate time for ECTs to ask questions, share their successes and express their frustrations and concerns. These communities work best if ECTs are confident that they are within a safe and confidential environment where their views will not be reported back to schools.

There is also an important role that needs to be handled with sensitivity and respect by the adviser in facilitating such wider communities. Each ECT's experience will be hugely influenced by their first educational setting and its context. Exposure to the wide variety of contexts and professional approaches across the system is vital to developing the awareness of the early professional. Here, as elsewhere, the role of the adviser is not to advocate for particular approaches of personal preferences but rather to raise awareness of the choices and ranges of evidence-informed possibilities in a rich educational landscape. Education advisers have the advantageous position of being emotionally removed from the day-to-day workings of any particular school and can explore some of the big challenges of our current system in addressing matters of pedagogy, curriculum, inclusion and equality. Helping our newest teachers to think about what is currently common practice and what innovations are possible is an important part of nurturing this community of early professionals.

Conclusion

In their first years in the profession, ECTs are often overwhelmed by the realisation that they are now responsible for a class of children and all that this entails. They need to be supported to navigate a clear pathway, with achievable steps, to an end goal. They also need a sense of collective purpose and to develop values that add to and learn from those already held within the community of the school.

It remains my belief that, as a profession, we can change the tide for the recruitment and retention of teachers by providing ECTs with a bespoke, supportive environment where their contribution is valued and expectations, while high, are also realistic. This is possible by first ensuring that, as education advisers, we support school leaders to evaluate whether their school setting has sufficient capacity to offer the nurturing environment required and give some ongoing independent verification. This is further enhanced by helping to facilitate and engage wider communities beyond the school. With this twofold approach, ECTs are given the best chance to create their own sense of belonging and value. Our role is also to support ECTs to realise and appreciate that they are in a unique and treasured position to make a positive impact, and often create a life-changing experience, for all the children in their care.

Further reading

Ambition Institute (England) (2024) *Early Career Teachers*. London: Ambition Institute.

Department for Education (England) (2019) *Early Career Framework*. London: UK Government.

Matila, M (2023) How England Lost Its Teachers – and How It Can Get Them Back. *Times Educational Supplement*, December. [online] Available at: www.tes.com/magazine/analysis/general/teacher-recruitment-retention-crisis-solution (accessed 29 June 2024).

Ovenden-Hope, T (2023) The Great Supply Crisis: Can the Early Career Framework Appease Early Career Teacher Recruitment and Retention Challenges in England?' *Impact*, January. [online] Available at: https://my.chartered.college/impact_article/the-great-supply-crisis-can-the-early-career-framework-appease-early-career-teacher-recruitment-and-retention-challenges-in-england (accessed 29 June 2024).

 References

Department for Education (England) (2021) *Teachers' Standards*. London: UK Government.

Lenning, O and Ebbers, L (1999) *The Powerful Potential of Learning Communities: Improving Education for the Future*. Washington, DC: George Washington University, Graduate School of Education and Human Development.

Worth, J and Faulkner-Ellis, H (2022) *Teacher Supply and Shortages: The Implications of Teacher Supply Challenges for Schools and Pupils*. London: National Foundation for Educational Research. [online] Available at: www.nfer.ac.uk/publications/teacher-supply-and-shortages-the-implications-of-teacher-supply-challenges-for-schools-and-pupils (accessed 29 June 2024).

10 Building capacity through a community of schools in a multi-academy trust

NARINDER GILL

Key learning

- Prepare the groundwork. Ensure a strong understanding of the why, what and how through intentional listening, transparent communication and stakeholder engagement. This approach gathers valuable data, builds relationships and creates readiness for change.

- Foster ownership. Develop a planned approach to cultivate a culture of ownership rather than dependency, avoiding learned helplessness. Being aware of red flags at the start of the journey helps to identify potential challenges.

- Provide focus and clarity. Stay focused on the main objectives. Distractions can divert resources and energy away from the core mission. Collaboration and a sense of belonging contribute to maintaining clarity.

- Continuously self-evaluate and adapt. Throughout the improvement journey, actively seek feedback and involve a good cross-section of stakeholder voices. This adaptability ensures responsiveness to changing needs. A willingness to quit systems that are not working demonstrates a commitment to improvement.

- Sustain commitment to looking beyond the trust and remain outward looking. Recognise the benefits of external expertise, learning from beyond the multi-academy trust.

AoEA criteria

- Criterion 6: Working in concert with the school's leadership

- Criterion 8: Understanding of causal factors impacting on school performance

- Criterion 10: Providing critical evaluation of the quality of leadership

- Criterion 11: Providing critical evaluation of the quality of teaching

- Criterion 13: Providing critical evaluation of collaborative working between governors, leaders and staff

- Criterion 14: Having an up-to-date knowledge of relevant educational policy, inspection and other related issues

Introduction

In the ever-evolving landscape of education, achieving excellence requires a deliberate collaborative effort. Elevate Multi-Academy Trust (MAT) embarked on this journey with a vision to build capacity through a community of schools. This chapter explores the strategies and initiatives employed by Elevate MAT to foster collaboration, empower educators and drive positive change across its network through systematic school improvement functions.

Context and vision

Founded in 2017, Elevate MAT encompasses primary schools across North Yorkshire and Leeds, aiming to ensure all pupils can aspire and achieve their full potential. Each school's unique identity and strong community ties are integral to our ethos, which emphasises the power of collaborative working and a positive culture.

Strategic initiatives for capacity building

As Elevate MAT expanded in 2019 and I took on my role as School Improvement Director, we recognised the need to strengthen partnerships and develop systems where collective purpose and direction fostered self-sustaining behaviours and increased leadership capacity.

Developing a shared language and purpose

In 2021, Steve Munby helped to catalyse our efforts by sharing his insights on authentic leadership from his book *'Imperfect Leadership'* (2019). This grounded our thinking around alignment, efficiency through standardisation and empowerment. He shared with leaders the importance of authentic and self-aware leadership in the face of challenges and political pressures, and challenged us to think deeply about working together for all children, utilising joint resources as opposed to competing for resources.

Establishing a coaching culture

The development of a coaching culture as a core intervention for unlocking potential and empowering leaders created the catalyst for change. We implemented:

- an Institute of Leadership and Management (ILM) accredited coaching programme for all headteachers;
- a 'CollectiveED Coaching, Mentoring and Professional Learning Award' with Leeds Beckett University;
- group supervision for all headteachers;
- a reflective space for all staff to attend to pause, reflect and re-balance.

Key findings from external evaluation of impact

Headteachers benefited from collaborative coaching, enhancing relationships across the trust.

- Coaching helped to foster leaders' self-reflection, reducing the pressure to have all the answers, and with an emphasis on empowering and enabling others.
- The cultural shift towards ethical leadership and well-being was evident, with strong buy-in from headteachers.

Systematic school improvement model

Leveraging experiences from coaching high-performance professionals in other sectors, I developed a school improvement strategy that was both systematic and flexible. This sought to define, track and evaluate. Each school's performance was meticulously monitored, with tailored tools for improvement based on urgency and need.

Enhancing team expertise and understanding

We enhanced our team's expertise in school improvement roles, significantly impacting on our schools. This development involved distinguishing the nuances of leadership across several schools from leading a single school. Often, leaders may apply strategies successful in their own schools to others without fully understanding the unique and varying contexts, which can lead to biases and ineffective support. Our approach ensures that leaders truly understand each school before implementing tailored support packages.

All our team members are working towards their Associate Accreditation with the AoEA, demonstrating their commitment to advancing their expertise in diverse school settings. The training fosters open-mindedness and a culture of curiosity, essential for effective school improvement. By shadowing each other and engaging in rich discussions, we have refined our approach to planning and capacity development. Team reflections emphasise balancing rapid improvement with a deep understanding of existing school structures, identifying what can be developed further and prioritising urgent needs.

We have developed a framework centred on the question, 'If I bring my expertise to this school, what will it look like and what will the impact be?' Our work at Elevate as advisers is guided by clearly defined milestones and success metrics, grounded in the capacity-building efforts we implement to empower school staff. However, this only comes alive through asking the right questions and having the right conversations to gain reliable information to understand what is needed.

Reflections from the School Improvement (SI) team:

> *The Trust's SI strategy clarifies the level and frequency of support, tailored to each school's unique needs based on data and staffing information. This clarity enables me, as the SI lead, to provide bespoke and impactful support. The role's capacity has been enhanced through continuous professional development (CPD) and shadowing experienced SI colleagues. Our targets have evolved with our growing expertise, ensuring schools achieve their goals within defined timelines, thus maintaining a cycle of progress, success celebration, and future improvement planning.*
>
> (Alex Hope, 2024)
>
> *As part of our commitment to our church schools, we have appointed a school improvement lead to facilitate their development and support. This role includes training to become a SIAMS (Statutory Inspection of Anglican and Methodist Schools) inspector and collaboration with diocesan advisers. The church school improvement lead co-ordinates efforts across two dioceses, fostering a collaborative environment among the seven schools. Initially focused on sharing best practices, this collaboration has evolved into a conference providing high quality religious education (RE) training for all staff. This comprehensive training approach ensures all staff in our church schools are equipped to recognise and implement good practice, setting a benchmark for ongoing high-quality CPD.*
>
> (Abi Clay, 2024)

Further enhancing team expertise

A key feature of our team's development has been maintaining an outward-facing perspective, actively listening and working cohesively. Team members are also pursuing the National Professional Qualification for Executive Leadership (NPQEL), and we have created shared documents to establish a common language and ensure consistent, high-quality support across all schools. A recent trip to a trust in Bristol, facilitated by Mick Waters, provided fresh perspectives and further sharpened our school improvement strategies.

Recognising the complexity of school improvement, we plan dedicated time for deep thinking and analysis, avoiding linear plans and instead delving into rich data sources to tailor our support effectively. If leaders are to accurately map what is going on in schools, they need to ask the right questions and have the right conversations. We want conversations to yield information that is as reliable as possible and that can be acted upon.

> As a new team member, I have benefited from the expertise and generosity of experienced colleagues, who have integrated me into the Elevate team. From the outset, I have participated in strategic planning for various school improvement aspects, such as academic achievement and teacher development. Collaborating with leading experts, I have contributed to planning professional development for staff. My experiences with other multi-academy trusts have brought fresh perspectives to our problem-solving approaches.
>
> (Emma Meadus, 2024)

Through these efforts, we have fine-tuned our support strategies, recognising the importance of understanding the specific needs of each school and ensuring our actions are purposeful and impactful. This continuous development of our adviser role underscores our commitment to providing high-quality education and fostering school improvement across our trust.

Working on agreed trust priorities

School improvement at scale is more than the enactment of identified initiatives. The planning that needed to take place involved many meetings and reframing.

Our thinking was challenged by an external consultant, who coached me to consider a basic process for improvement that I believe enabled us to further build a culture and connected everyone to the shared purpose. Looking at the recent Education Endowment Foundation (EEF) guidance 2024 and the social aspect of effective improvement, we sought to elaborate on the:

- Why? Why are we looking to do this?
- What? What, exactly, will we have achieved once we have achieved success?
- How? How will we ensure we are successful?

Robinson (2017) states that leaders *'need to be increasingly knowledgeable about the core business of teaching, learning, assessment and curriculum. And they need to be able to use that knowledge to make good decisions'* (para 15). She also states (Robinson, 2010) that leaders use *'content knowledge to solve complex school-based problems, while building relational trust with staff, parents, and students'* (p 5).

Drawing from Robinson's insights on content knowledge and relational trust, we focused on two key initiatives using our basic process for improvement:

1. *Creating a trust curriculum grounded in design principles.* We collectively built knowledge and expertise, influencing and learning from one another in a community of improvement. Professional conversations replaced checklists, fostering genuine collaboration.

2. *Implementing a teaching and learning framework.* Central to our vision for excellence, this framework emphasised consistency, excellence and continuous improvement. A phased implementation plan included training, quality assurance and ongoing support, ensuring every educator was equipped to deliver high-quality teaching. In our work with Elevate MAT, we have ensured a consistent approach to pedagogy by involving all

Introduction: creating a shared framework for learning	Applications for appointments of leaders of education who formed the working group to develop the framework	Working with external expertise to explore evidence, clarify understanding and create a draft framework	Stakeholders are consulted to review draft framework	Trust staff engagement and feedback is used to refine framework and train the trainer workshops	Implementation of framework and train the trainer programme in place
Headteacher conference May 2022	**June 2022**	**Sept – February 2023**	**February 2023**	**March 2023**	**Sept 2023**

Figure 10.1: Development stages to launch

teachers and teaching assistants in the trust. This process has been carefully thought through, recognising that each stage (Figure 10.1) will take the time necessary to lead to positive engagement, further innovation and ownership by all schools.

Over time, we have developed this offer based upon local needs and national initiatives and harnessed a career framework from ITT students to executive headteacher roles within the trust. This has enabled us to recruit from within and succession plan with confidence, further developing our capacity to sustain improvement. Recent research nationally shows that just 6 per cent of teachers feel a sense of belonging to their trust. It is our duty, we believe, to create a trust where everyone feels valued and empowered, and has bought into the shared vision and values of the trust.

The following diagram is an example of how we, as a community of schools, are beginning to ensure we are clear on why we are doing what we are doing to improve schools across the trust.

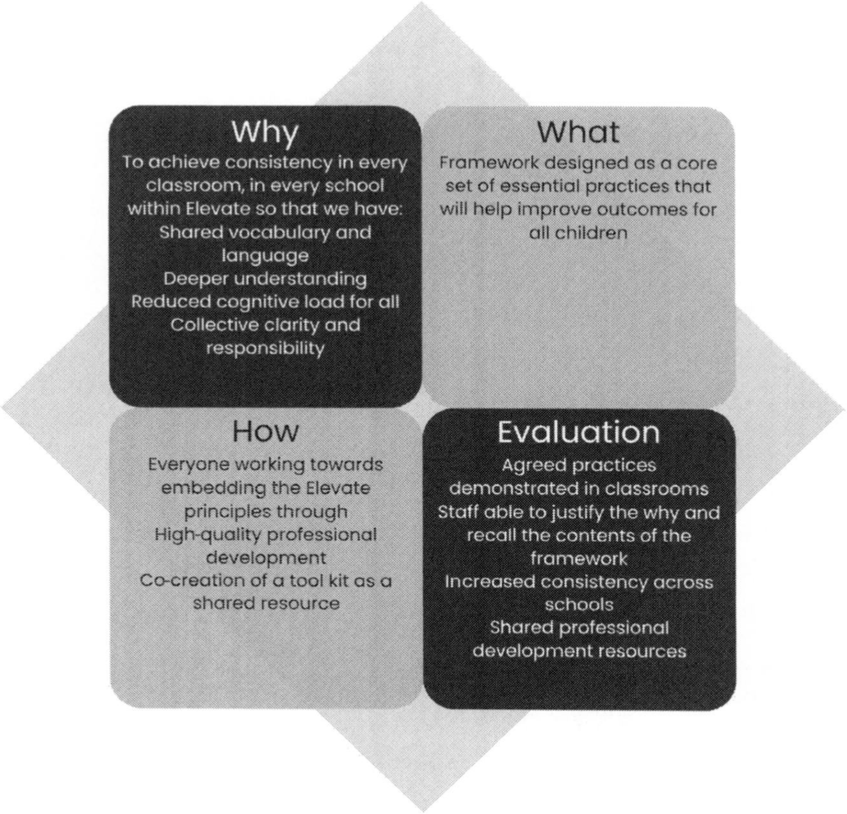

Why
To achieve consistency in every classroom, in every school within Elevate so that we have:
Shared vocabulary and language
Deeper understanding
Reduced cognitive load for all
Collective clarity and responsibility

What
Framework designed as a core set of essential practices that will help improve outcomes for all children

How
Everyone working towards embedding the Elevate principles through
High-quality professional development
Co-creation of a tool kit as a shared resource

Evaluation
Agreed practices demonstrated in classrooms
Staff able to justify the why and recall the contents of the framework
Increased consistency across schools
Shared professional development resources

Figure 10.2: How we ensure that we are clear on why we are doing what we are doing

Key actions that supported implementation and enabled schools to embed and sustain improvements included:

- train the trainer material created for each principle (based on research and evidence);
- two headteachers trained as trainers;
- video of training created to reinforce messages;
- key priority included in the School Development Plan (SDP) and performance development target 2 for headteachers and teachers;

- a central resource portal of all materials created on Microsoft Teams;
- a planned programme to develop teaching assistants' expertise in scaffolding children's learning. This started with a teaching assistants' conference followed by two teaching assistants from each school becoming leads. The teaching assistants were further supported by membership of the Chartered College of Teaching.

Progress and impact to date has included:

- Consistent messages shared during training of each principle across the trust.
- Capacity increased to deliver consistent training across all schools.
- All staff across the trust having now had the training – teachers and teaching assistants – and they now understand expectations for each principle.
- Headteachers having a clear action plan for implementing and embedding the principles across each classroom.
- Headteachers having audited their own specific areas for development against the Teaching Learning and Assessment (TLA) principles.
- School improvement now focused upon key areas to support and a shared language leading to increased outcomes.
- Staff are now sharing more among themselves.

A headteacher who has led on this said:

> *Supporting the implementation of the TLA was a great opportunity to be at the forefront of a significant trust priority. It allowed me to shape the principles, training and implementation into what I thought would best help the trust schools. This would further strengthen the implementation of the TLA principles in my school as I was already fully invested in these and therefore it would make it more impactful when my staff were receiving the training and also prioritising the*

→

development of specific principles. Completing the NPQEL alongside supporting the trust schools with the TLA gave me a greater insight into what it takes to be a trust leader as the NPQEL training focused heavily on the development of a wider community of schools and not just our own.

(Steve Butterworth, 2024)

Conclusion

The journey towards building capacity through a community of schools in our multi-academy trust is characterised by collaboration, innovation and a relentless commitment to excellence. Through our coaching culture development, curriculum co-creation, teaching and learning framework, implementation and assessment integration, Elevate MAT has demonstrated its dedication to empowering educators, supporting success and driving positive change across its family of schools. In addition to fostering a culture of collaboration and excellence, Elevate MAT has strategically invested in leadership development to drive school improvement at scale. Through targeted training and support, leaders within the trust have been equipped with the knowledge, skills and mindset necessary to lead and support schools effectively – even from afar. This investment in leadership development has been instrumental in building capacity within schools and empowering leaders to navigate complex challenges with empathy, insight and strategic foresight.

 Further reading

Sharples, J, Eaton, J and Boughelaf, J (2024) *A School's Guide to Implementation*. London: Education Endowment Foundation.

References

Munby, S (2019) *Imperfect Leadership*. Carmarthen: Crown House.

Robinson, V (2010) From Instructional Leadership to Leadership Capabilities: Empirical Findings and Methodological Challenges. *Leadership and Policy in Schools*, 9(1): 1–26.

Robinson, V (2017) Leadership Q&A with Viviane Robinson. *Teacher Bulletin*, 2 August.

11 Seeing the school through the headteacher's eyes: unlocking and strengthening the capacity for sustainable improvement at school level and for a system of schools

IAN LANE

Key learning

- People are born wanting to learn and wanting to do a good job. They are naturally, intrinsically motivated – none more so than the headteacher.

- Building trust and taking the time to see a school through the head's eyes will encourage openness, a shared understanding of the 'reality' and a more emotionally energised engagement with a process of continuous improvement.

- An empathic, discerning external pair of eyes can be an effective mechanism for both the school and the provider in unlocking and in strengthening the capacity for sustainable change and improvement.

- The support and challenge function should be a shared focus between two peers, both of whom invest in and seek to provide the best possible education and life chances for the school's and the system of schools' children and young people.

AoEA criteria

- Criterion 6: Working in concert with the school's leadership

- Criterion 7: Providing clear, insightful and well-written reports

- Criterion 8: Understanding of causal factors impacting on school improvement

- Criterion 10: Providing critical evaluation of the quality of leadership

- Criterion 13: Providing critical evaluation of collaborative working between governors, leaders and staff

- Criterion 14: Having an up-to-date knowledge of relevant educational policy, inspection and other related issues

Introduction

This chapter is underpinned by the belief that people are born wanting to learn and that they want to 'do a good job' – none more so than the headteacher. In fact, I don't think I have ever met any headteachers that turn up for work wanting to get it wrong. Even those we rarely encounter that say they can't or won't still want to get it right.

Some years ago, I was appointed as a senior education adviser by an 'outward-facing' and extremely able head of school improvement, who afforded me the opportunity to work in another local authority as part of a team of external school improvement partners (SIPs). The role was part of the government's 'A New Relationship with Schools', referred to by Kevin McDermid in Chapter 3 of the first book in this series, *The Role of the Education Adviser*. Like Kevin and all other soon-to-be SIPs at the time, I duly undertook the SIP national accreditation. The remit for this role, funded by the government but commissioned via local authorities for all state-funded schools, had been clearly established and was well articulated in *The School Improvement Partner's Brief*, published at the time:

- *focus on pupil progress and attainment across the ability range*, and the many factors which influence it, including pupil well-being, extended services and parental involvement;

- *respect for the school's autonomy to plan its development*, starting from the school's self-evaluation and the needs of the pupils and of other members of the school community;

- *professional challenge and support*, so the school's practice and performance are improved; and

- *evidence-based assessment* of the school's performance and its strategies for improving teaching and learning.

The commissioning local authority also provided SIPs with locally held school and national key data sets, as well as the most recent inspection report. It was at the time in England when Fischer Family Trust (FFT) contextual value added (CVA) data were gaining some traction with schools and local authorities, since this data set went some way towards recognising key contextual differences between schools. However, the stakes were still high and, for SIPs working with schools, there remained a need to convince headteachers that the 'partner' in 'school improvement partner' was more than a 'trendy' shift in national policy.

Seeing the school through the head's eyes

So there I was, provided with the local authority's information about the school, about to make my first ever SIP visit. When I looked at the data for this school, I was somewhat shocked. The school's data was a 'sea of blue'. Blue was the equivalent of poor performance and, to add insult to injury, the blue was also supported with percentile rankings for all measures, which were mainly at the 99th or the 100th percentile! Knowing the inspection framework, I was also puzzled at how, with this data, the school could have possibly been judged 'satisfactory' and not 'inadequate' at its most recent inspection. I could imagine what the headteacher might have said had I begun the visit by challenging that judgement and sought to scrutinise more closely the correlation between performance and the inspection report. Having consulted my SIP co-ordinator and 'thanked' him for allocating me the school, I decided that the data would be the last port of call for our first encounter.

On arriving at the school, I was met with a beaming smile from the receptionist, had my ID and safeguarding documentation checked and was met promptly in person by the headteacher. There was clearly going to be more to what was going on in this school than I had originally anticipated. First impressions do matter and, more often than not, are a good indicator of what is likely to follow. We began the day with a short conversation in the headteacher's office during which I made clear that, while I had had the chance to scrutinise the school's performance data, I was keen to get to know and see the school through his eyes. He was initially a little surprised and was probably expecting the usual barrage of questions in relation to the school's poor performance. He was delighted to oblige, so we set off.

Of course, this approach allowed me to begin to build a relationship with the headteacher, see the school at work and then hear and learn so much more about the school. For the most part, I saw orderly behaviour and a good level of engagement in lessons. The learning environment was pristine, with student work being prominently and proudly displayed. Relationships between the headteacher and the staff were positive and mutually respectful, as they were with students and between students. Where, on a rare occasion, the headteacher needed to intervene and assert his authority, the response from students was immediate and compliant. As we toured the school, dialogue became increasingly less guarded and the headteacher's high aspirations for the young people in his care were palpable.

During and following our tour of the school, we were able to reflect on what we had seen and, even more importantly, what we hadn't seen. Challenges in relation to leadership and performance were openly shared, as were legacy issues in relation to performance, leadership and governance. There was honesty in relation to the strengths and shortcomings of the school, and of local authority support and collaborative working. We were then able to begin to 'dig deeper' and relate the data to the current reality. While there were significant challenges in relation to performance, we were nevertheless looking at 'lag indicators', some of which were already being addressed.

This headteacher, with his team and now supported by a more enlightened governing body, was attempting to do all the right things in the right order but he knew he couldn't do it on his own. He needed a team both outside and within the school, and he wanted me as an invaluable part of that wider strategic team and improvement function. I was part of the 'supportive intervention' invited to challenge, which Les Walton refers to in Chapter 6 in our first book in the series.

Curriculum and both senior and middle leadership were key areas of focus. He removed, and I helped to enable the removal of, several barriers along the way and the school improved year on year, facilitated by a mature evidence-led and outcome-driven school improvement partnership process. Outcomes for the school improved exponentially in both value-added scores and in key threshold measures. Inspection reports confirmed the strengthened capacity of leadership, the pace of improvement and the high quality of education, with the school also ranked as one of the top 15 most improved schools nationally.

Although I was working with a confident and able leader, listening to and 'seeing the school through the head's eyes' – at least initially in my experience – works equally well with a less experienced headteacher or even one who is reluctant to engage. In whatever way this initial point of contact and subsequent discussions pan out, the headteacher's insight helps to shed light on the working relationship that needs to ensue, the priorities for improvement that need to be focused on and the emotionally intelligent skillset that needs to be exercised to best engage the leader in working through a well-evidenced cycle of continuous improvement.

Impact on the system of schools locally

There was clearly power in this way of working for both the system of schools locally and for the individual school. As a SIP working within a local authority, I was able to derive a deep understanding of the challenges facing my own cross-section of schools and, in this role, work with the local authority and the SIP team to support an increasingly well-informed school improvement collaborative across the partnership of schools. It was, and felt, both sharply focused and 'bottom-up', as if the system were really listening to its leaders – as well as, when needed, constructively challenging them.

As a senior local authority adviser, I was also able to share with this local authority some excellent practice from our own local authority of schools, which was validated by our SIPs, as well as facilitate links between schools across the two local authorities and beyond because of the wider, more structured opportunity to network with other school improvement professionals through the SIP programme. We were all 'tapping into' one another's strengths and developing our own and one another's capacity to improve. We were becoming a more sharply focused, self-improving system.

As a local authority ourselves, we had regular, well-structured meetings with our SIPs. This broadly followed the support and challenge elements of the improvement cycle: evaluation of performance, target-setting, advising governors on the performance management of the headteacher, self-evaluation, improvement planning, and the monitoring and evaluation of implementation. This improvement cycle was supported by well-written, evidence-informed reports for both the local authority and governors. The structure was helpful but fluid enough not to be constraining. The intelligence we had on our own local authority schools enabled us to learn from each other, address weaknesses and procure well-targeted professional learning from one another's schools as a key feature of school leaders' meetings. These meetings were facilitated by the local authority, although they were school-led and chaired, replicating at a partnership level the commitment to school-led capacity building and improvement.

As a local authority , we had been part of the national 'Trials' programme for SIPs, and the local authority had decided to commission its SIP function from a highly reputable organisation comprising some of the country's leading school improvement specialists, all of whom had enjoyed significant success as headteachers themselves. The involvement of the external provider proved to be priceless in enabling well-focused partnership working between schools with the local authority.

Although commissioned by the local authority, part of our SIPs' remit was to challenge both the local authority and the school for the part each was playing in enabling effective partnership working. This assisted us as a local authority in improving our own support and challenge functions, added capacity at a strategic level and a deeper, more insightful commitment to collaboration for all schools – for those deemed to be high performing and those less so – in their aspirations to be as good as they possibly could be. We saw year-on-year improvement in results, in inspection outcomes and in the rating of Children's Services, which went from a poor satisfactory to excellent. While it is difficult to claim that all of this was down to an improved advisory function, it was clearly a contributory factor and the 'buy in' from both primary and secondary schools was fulsome and focused.

Impact on the school system as a whole

'A New Relationship with Schools' brought with it a healthy rethink nationally in relation to how schools and their leaders might best be supported to improve. It placed the headteacher at the heart of the school's own improvement and sought to bring critical friendship and an empathic challenge to the process. Local authorities still had their powers to intervene if schools that were underperforming didn't 'buy in', and many local authorities exercised this function well, deploying additional resources – often from one of their own schools – to effect improvement. The government department with the responsibility for education also had powers to intervene with local authorities if any of a local authority's schools were deemed to be 'failing'. Overall, there seemed to be a genuine attempt to establish the right balance between support and challenge.

Regionally and locally, there was an infrastructure of support for improvement through National Strategies with national strategies consultants deployed within local authorities to support professional learning. Support for improvement at both a local and regional level varied in terms of its quality, and sometimes it was seen as being too prescriptive. Nevertheless, there was an attempt to provide a nationally co-ordinated support infrastructure as a counter-balance to the accountability. There was regular dialogue with local authorities at a regional level and helpful updates and communication in relation to national policy direction. There was also some attempt to focus inspection on the school's own self-evaluation, although in reality inspection outcomes were still largely informed by results and 'lag' indicators.

Conclusion

Many would argue that, with 'A New Relationship with Schools', we were close to establishing a system-wide listening culture that was enabling and empowering headteachers to affect their own and one another's school improvement priorities. The NFER Evaluation of the SIP Trials Programme also came up with some interesting evidence to support this way of working with headteachers, and found that around 90 per cent of primary respondents strongly agreed, or agreed that their SIP was 'helpful', challenging', 'supportive', 'easy to talk to', 'has the right level of experience/knowledge' and 'is very good at dealing with data' ... and over 90 per cent of secondary respondents strongly agreed or agreed that their SIP was 'helpful', 'supportive', 'easy to talk to', 'has the right level of experience / knowledge' and 'is very good at dealing with data'.

Any national programme runs the risk of simplifying responses to issues that are not deeply enough understood at a local level. Headteachers, no matter where they work, and irrespective of the size or type of school they lead, should be entitled to be listened to and supported in addressing their school's unique needs and challenges. This should begin with the school's own self-evaluation and prioritisation, which is then supported and challenged through a rigorous, though genuine, partnership process with a view to embedding a cycle of continuous improvement. Many education advisers are assisting schools and partnerships of schools in achieving this. A good number of these advisers are part of a growing network of accredited associates and senior associates of the AoEA.

 Further reading

Atkinson, K, Judkins, M, Halsey, K and Rudd, P (2005) *New Relationship with Schools: Evaluation of Trial Local Authorities and School.* London: National Foundation of Education of Research for the Department of Education and Skills.

$\longrightarrow$

Department for Education (2006) *School Improvement Partner Programme: Advice and Guidance for Local Authorities.* London: UK Government.

Department for Education and Skills (2004) *A New Relationship with Schools.* London: UK Government.

Department of Education and Skills (nd) *A New Relationship with Schools: A School Improvement Partner's Brief.* London: National Foundation of Education of Research for the Department of Education and Skills.

12 Capacity-building through a strategic, well-prioritised school improvement plan

PETER PARISH

Key learning

- A well-prioritised school improvement plan is central to facilitating monitoring, self-evaluation and accountability.

- The adviser should ensure that ownership of the plan rests with the senior leadership and governors, and that it is shared with staff.

- All staff should be involved in some way in co-constructing the plan.

- Strategic planning requires a longer-term view.

AoEA criteria

- Criterion 6: Working in concert with the school's leadership

- Criterion 7: Providing clear, insightful and well-written reports

- Criterion 8: Understanding of causal factors impacting on school performance

- Criterion 9: Providing critical evaluation of performance

- Criterion 10: Providing critical evaluation of the quality of leadership

- Criterion 13: Providing critical evaluation of collaborative working between governors, leaders and staff

- Criterion 14: Having an up-to-date knowledge of relevant educational policy and other related issues

Introduction

One way or another, I have been involved in improvement planning for most of my career. This improvement planning has spanned the development of advisory service plans, children's services plans, council-wide corporate plans, school improvement plans and post-Ofsted action plans. I also have the privilege of reading many of the case studies presented by AoEA Associates in their portfolios, in many cases giving examples of how they intervened when things – including improvement planning – went disastrously wrong. This chapter focuses on strategic school improvement planning and its contribution to building capacity.

There probably isn't much new in improvement planning, as much of what constitutes good practice has been known for a long time. I was involved in a project which led to the publication *How to Write a School Development Plan* (Rogers, 1994). What is surprising is the number of times recognised good practice is ignored, leading to an inevitable downfall – often courtesy of external inspectors. For instance, the head who decided to write the plan on his own and keep it in his office so nobody else got sight of it. Or the school where curriculum managers did their own thing, using their own format, thus having no effective systems for whole-school monitoring and accountability. Other examples include improvement plans with so many actions and targets that staff feel overloaded and cannot grasp what the key priorities are.

Those working in an advisory capacity might be called upon to support the writing of plans in a variety of contexts, such as:

- school improvement planning, as part of the school's annual improvement planning cycle;
- post-inspection planning;
- corporate or strategic planning;
- action plan sections for bids or proposals;
- premises development;
- conversion to academies or the formation of academy trusts or collaborative federations.

Many of these involve plans that span short periods of time, often covering a single year. Strategic improvement planning involves a longer timeframe and focuses on achieving a vision over several years.

As an example, a school in an area of social disadvantage had a plan to achieve a long-term vision to build the profile of the school through community engagement over several years. Another example is a school whose pupil profile was changing significantly; as a result, plans needed to include special needs-resourced provision. This process depended on building support with the community and the funding authority to achieve the high educational standards to which the school's leadership aspired for all learners. A further example is a school whose new leadership aimed to go from underperforming to outstanding, a process that needed planning over several years and involved restructuring of responsibilities, targeted professional learning for staff and improved systems for pupil progress monitoring, coupled with improved IT systems.

An effective strategic improvement plan can be a powerful way of communicating strategic direction and priorities. It is also the cornerstone for monitoring and accountability.

Strategic improvement planning in a nutshell

Strategic improvement planning is a process that allows school leaders to map out their vision for the school's growth and how they are going to achieve it. A strategic improvement plan can be a significant aid to the leadership, by communicating the direction of travel, highlighting priorities that facilitate focused high-quality professional development and rigorous performance management of staff – all of which increase the capacity for consistent and sustained whole-school improvement.

To be properly strategic, improvement plans need to be able to focus on the medium to longer term, as well as dealing with the immediate year ahead. To get that longer term focus, as Stephen Covey says, we should begin with the end in mind (2020). The immediate plan focusing on the year ahead will be more detailed whereas the medium-term plan will be less detailed and outline priorities over the next two to three years. The longer-term plans might stretch to five years and beyond and will inevitably be less detailed still but will set a general direction of travel and will cover elements of the school's strategic development. For instance, considering pupil admission projection data, is the school roll likely to be expanding or contracting and what are the implications of and possible mitigations against any risks? Perhaps the nature of the school's intake is changing – for instance, more pupils with special educational or behavioural needs requiring the development of specialist or resourced provision, which in turn will have capital implications requiring discussion and proposals to the appropriate funding agency. Trends in digital learning might need to be reflected in medium-term planning and include professional learning, the acquisition of IT equipment and software, and modification of premises.

Adviser involvement

The nature of the adviser's involvement in the strategic improvement planning process is likely to be dependent on their or their commissioners' perceptions of the quality of school leadership. When working with a high-performing leadership team, it is likely to be about scrutinising plans and challenging the targets that have been set. For schools where the principal is new in their post and inexperienced, the role is likely to involve an element of coaching and/or mentoring. With a school considered to be coasting or underperforming, the challenge may well be more directive. Where a school is judged to be failing, the adviser's input might be through the equivalent of an interim executive board, which will plan and put more robust systems in place and may even be instrumental in replacing the principal. In these circumstances, the adviser is likely to have a much greater role in writing the strategic improvement plan.

Engaging all appropriately in a process of change

It is important that the ownership of the improvement plan rests with the school leadership and governors. A plan that is not owned by the school will not provide sustainable improvement in the long run. The adviser can challenge, give advice and suggestions, provide examples and point out the implications from reviewing data, but normally must resist the temptation to write the plan for the school.

Ultimately, the central purpose of any improvement plan must be to improve outcomes for all children and young people in the care of the school. Often this will be encapsulated in a vision or mission statement. All the time, the question needs to be asked: How does the plan help our pupils or students? This will also be a critical issue when it comes to setting performance measures in the plan.

The school should work to a common model for school improvement planning. The improvement planning process can be cascaded from the overarching strategic improvement plan to departmental or key stage plans, which follow the same format. This gives greater clarity to the planning process and helps to build capacity by making a wider group of staff familiar with the planning process, setting actions and targets, and using these for performance accountability.

Arriving at priorities

The adviser will rarely be involved in writing a strategic school improvement plan from scratch. They are most likely to be involved in reviewing and updating an existing plan. To provide an effective input, the adviser should start by reviewing or auditing existing information relating to the school and helping to answer the question 'Where are we now?' Obviously, key performance information will need to be analysed and the school's analysis scrutinised. These data should be supplemented by more qualitative forms of information such as that coming from pupil voice, staff perceptions, parental feedback and governors' views.

Identification of priorities is likely to start with the senior leadership team and key governors, such as the Chair; however, before firming up, it should progressively involve consultation with staff and the governing body.

The adviser could use several tools to suggest or clarify priorities. It might be useful to undertake a situational audit by applying a PESTLE analysis. PESTLE stands for Political, Economic, Social, Technological, Legal and Environmental. Strategic planners could consider how each of these facets might impact the school and need to be addressed. In many respects, it is a type of horizon scanning. For instance, changes in legislation might have implications for safeguarding practice. It can be helpful at the self-evaluation stage in terms of getting key governors and senior leaders together and drilling down. For example, does the curriculum teach statutory requirements in sufficient time? Is it affordable? Are staff being upskilled in the right areas, given those drivers for change?

Drawing on the data analysis, a SWOT analysis can also be helpful. Cross-referencing the SWOT analysis against a PESTLE analysis can help to set longer term priorities. The adviser can facilitate such exercises and help at intervals to summarise discussion. Another activity that we have used within the AoEA is an organisational climate analysis (we refer to it as 'Context for Organisational Improvement'). It can be used to assess the impact of leadership on climate by gauging staff perceptions of what it is like to work in the school and what, ideally, they would like it to be. This can be a useful aid to developing capacity.

The audit and situational analysis will lead to the identification of several priorities for improvement. These priorities should not be so numerous that the improvement plan becomes unwieldy and should focus on those things that are really important, thereby reducing the number of diversionary activities or projects that lead to effort being too thinly spread. Arriving at a sensible number of priorities can be helped by carrying out a paired comparisons exercise where each of the priorities is ranked against the others in order of importance.

Priorities are likely to be identified in relation to areas of school activity, such as:

- curriculum;

- teaching and learning;

- inclusion;

- safeguarding and pupil well-being;

- professional learning;
- learning environment.

Planning for each key identified area of provision should be supported by relevant quantitative and qualitative performance measures and should be informed by an analysis of the causes of any underperformance and specifically address these.

The best plans have clarity in alignment of performance in relation to the school's key performance indicators, with robust self-evaluation informed by performance evidence and aligned to regulatory inspection frameworks where these exist. These then link to sharply written plans that pick up on priorities for improvement, inclusive of any that inspectors have said need addressing, and link to evaluation of impact a year on, informing a subsequent cycle. This should result in actions that will be tested, monitored, reviewed and updated, leading to a kind of Kaizen type of cyclical process of continuous improvement planning.

The introduction to any strategic improvement plan should include an overview of the data analysis and research that have led to the plan's priorities.

Objectives to action

The identification of priorities should lead to the identification of key objectives that move the priorities into action. Objectives are precise measurable statements of intended outcomes, which specify intentions rather than actions. The objectives give clarity of purpose and outline the key task. They are strategic rather than focusing on day-to-day tasks. Actions to achieve the objective will then be outlined underneath the objective.

It can be useful to use Lewin's force field analysis to inform actions. The analysis highlights driving forces for change and key restraining forces that need to be addressed through actions to avoid undermining the broader strategy.

As mentioned earlier, action plans should have a common structure across the school so all those involved are working to common systems for monitoring and evaluation. This will also help to build capacity by developing a shared understanding of the improvement planning process. The adviser should check action plans to see whether they contain the right level of detail. Typically, actions planned under an objective should include the following information: action, start and finish dates, who is leading on the action, who is monitoring, milestones, the intended outcome and a column for progress.

Performance measures should relate to the headline objective, so it is not necessary to have lots of performance measures for individual actions, helping to ensure the strategy doesn't get lost in the detail.

Setting performance measures

I once reviewed a departmental improvement plan that had the action 'buy filing cabinet' and the success indicator was 'filing cabinet bought'. Although a trivial example, it raises an important point. What is the purpose of an improvement plan and who or what should be the focus of the plan? The plan's focus, and therefore its performance measures, should be about improving outcomes for children and young people. The question about focus should be asked repeatedly when reviewing or advising on plans.

In the early 2000s, many schools were involved with the 'Turning the Curve' project, which was based on the book *Trying Hard is Not Good Enough* by Mark Friedman (2015). The book and approach related to outcomes-based accountability. It asks three questions about what is important when assessing and monitoring performance:

- How much did we do?

- How well did we do it?

And crucially:

- Is anyone better off?

It is the last of these questions that should inform the setting of relevant performance measures.

Clear success criteria provide an aid to effective self-evaluation and progress reporting. They are also a significant aid to the governing body when carrying out its accountability function. In some cases, it might be necessary to work with the members of the governing body to help them understand their role and coach them in the type of questions to ask the leadership team when holding them to account. It can also be a good idea to encourage reporting of relevant aspects of the plan by middle leaders; this can help to develop leadership capacity within the school.

Reviewing the strategic improvement plan

Reviewing the plan involves two aspects. There is the overarching improvement plan review, in which the extent of achieving the success criteria is assessed. This will denote the end of the designated planning cycle – for instance, often reported on in September to reflect progress in the previous academic year. The progress of the plan will be reported to the governors, who should hold the school leadership to account for progress. As well as reviewing the extent of achieving the success criteria, the review should also consider the effectiveness of the strategy itself.

The strategic improvement planning process is not linear in nature. It should be dynamic and capable of being adjusted if evidence indicates that change is required. The school leadership should also be monitoring the plan in a day-to-day sense. The adviser might be called upon to contribute to monitoring of an aspect of the plan or to review the effectiveness of the leadership's monitoring. Outcomes of monitoring might provide the stimulus to update the plan. For instance, monitoring could highlight that a group of pupils have been underperforming and that actions might need to be changed.

In general, to make modification to the improvement plan manageable following monitoring, it is useful to schedule a time during the year to bring monitoring information together to update the plan. Such an interim review during the planning cycle is often known as a 'fixed-point review'. This is a useful way of checking progress and realigning the plan to remain on target rather than waiting until the end of the cycle only to discover the plan was not meeting the original objectives.

Conclusion

It is a good idea to have an executive summary of the strategic improvement plan. This will make it easier to communicate the key priorities and objectives. It will help staff and key stakeholders to understand and commit to the priorities and objectives.

An effective strategic improvement plan can set the road map for progressive improvement and growth, in terms of capacity, of the organisation to improve outcomes for the prime stakeholders: children and young people.

 Further reading

Department for Education (DFE) (2008) *Turning the Curve Stories*. London: UK Government.

 References

Covey, S R (2020) *The 7 Habits of Highly Effective People*. London: Simon & Schuster.

Friedman, M (2015) *Trying Hard is Not Good Enough*. CreateSpace.

Rogers, R (1994) *How to Write a School Development Plan*. London: Heinemann.

Part 3
Supporting collaborative school improvement

13 The role of advisers in promoting equity within education systems

PROFESSOR MEL AINSCOW, CBE

Key learning

- Analysis of context is key. While there will be some similarities in relation to causes of underperformance across schools, every school needs to be analysed in detail and to engage in a process of improvement to address their unique needs.

- Help is required to ensure that the school's leadership is acting with sufficient urgency in addressing priorities for improvement, drawing on the strengths of others from within the school to assist in that leadership.

- It is important to support the raising of expectations in relation to what it is possible to achieve, particularly in schools where there has been a legacy of underperformance.

- To avoid a feeling of isolation, particularly for schools facing significant challenge, schools should be connected discerningly with each other.

- In working across a partnership of schools, advisers should meet with and learn from each other, drawing on one another's knowledge of the schools, their strengths and collective resources.

AoEA criteria

- Criterion 6: Working in concert with the school's leadership

- Criterion 7: Providing clear, insightful and well-written reports

- Criterion 8: Understanding of causal factors impacting on school performance

- Criterion 9: Providing critical evaluation of performance

- Criterion 10: Providing critical evaluation of the quality of leadership

- Criterion 13: Providing critical evaluation of collaborative working between governors, leaders and staff

- Criterion 14: Having an up-to-date knowledge of relevant educational policy and other related issues

Introduction

Some years ago, I attended a meeting of local authority advisers as they debated their roles. When the discussion became rather heated, one member of the group commented: *'Look colleagues, this is simple: the job of schools is to improve themselves. Our job is to make sure it happens.'*

In this chapter, I consider what those who take on an advisory role with schools can contribute. I do this by reflecting on my work within two government-instigated improvement initiatives: the Greater Manchester Challenge, from 2007 to 2011; and Schools Challenge Cymru, from 2014 to 2017. Both projects involved teams of Challenge Advisers and focused on finding ways to break the link between disadvantaged home backgrounds and educational outcomes (Ainscow, Chapman and Hadfield, 2020).

Strategies

Within the two Challenge programmes, the aim was to 'get behind' people in schools, on the assumption that if they were to make progress, they would improve themselves. Analysis of context was crucial in this respect, the purpose being able to build on relative strengths within individual schools and address areas of their work that were a cause for concern.

One source of information regarding support was provided through the 'families of schools' data system, within which schools were grouped on the basis of the profiles of the communities they served (Ainscow, 2015). In this way, schools could compare their current levels of pupil achievement with those found in similar schools. They could also locate schools with relevant strengths that they might choose to approach for support.

Those schools facing particular challenges received more intensive support from a Challenge Adviser. Through their involvement in the process of assessing the context and formulating a plan of action, the Challenge Advisers were then able to evaluate whether other, more drastic actions were needed to secure the school's improvement. Of course, in some instances this might mean a decision that the head, or other senior staff, did not have the capabilities to lead the process.

Challenging contexts

The approach used in those schools facing challenging circumstances was based on a detailed analysis of the local context and the development of an improvement strategy that fitted these circumstances. The Challenge Advisers had a central role, working alongside senior school staff to carry out an analysis and mobilise external support where needed.

A common feature of almost all these interventions was that progress was achieved through carefully matching schools across social 'boundaries' of various kinds, including those between different local authorities. In this way, expertise that previously had been trapped in particular contexts was made more widely available.

Crossing boundaries sometimes involved what seemed like unlikely partnerships. For example, a highly successful primary school catering for children from Jewish Orthodox families worked with an inner-city school working mainly with Muslim children to develop more effective use of assessment data and boost the quality of teaching and learning. Another unusual partnership involved a primary school that had developed considerable expertise in teaching children to read in supporting a secondary school in another local authority where low levels of literacy had acted as a barrier to student progress.

Supporting improvements

The approaches used by the Challenge Advisers to support the process of change varied from school to school. Nevertheless, an overall pattern guided these interventions. This was helpfully summed up in a set of notes written by one of the Challenge Advisers. He wrote:

The following is a brief reflection on the process I engage with while working as a Challenge Adviser. Whilst it is written as a linear process, in practice it was never like this. That said, I feel the following is a useful and authentic guide to what happened when working with challenging schools.

Step 1. An initial review process using key documents and data. This involved working with senior local authority colleagues to carry out a review to ensure the right schools were targeted for involvement. Having identified schools for involvement, I carried out a review, using statistical evidence, inspection reports, local authority and internal evaluations, to achieve an overview of the quality and effectiveness of individual schools.

Step 2. Establish a framework for the improvement process. This involved me in working with the leadership of each school in carrying out an inquiry in order to establish improvement targets, proposed actions, intended outcomes and a timescale for completion. This was supported by systematic quality assurance to ensure standards were being achieved and accountability was real. Due to the nature and speed of change, this was a constant and cyclical activity within the improvement drive.

Step 3. Implement activities to impact on the priority areas. Whilst the targets for most schools tended to fall within the areas of leadership, learning, teaching and community, there was a drive to ensure they were relevant to the particular context and tightly focused. In response to these targets, working with colleagues was crucial, such as colleagues from within the Challenge team and the local authority, in deciding what the support package should be for each school and when it should be deployed.

Step 4. Support, challenge and manage the development of improvement activities. This was crucial to ensure that: the change process was being managed effectively; each school turned its plan into actions, making and consolidating progress as appropriate; there was systematic monitoring of the impact of all aspects of the support package and the contributions of stakeholders; and there was effective monitoring of school performance to ensure targets were being achieved.

Step 5. Effective reporting procedures. These were intended to ensure that stakeholders were informed of all aspects of progress at the individual and authority level. As part of my routine work, after each school visit I completed a 'note of visit', which highlighted progress with specific reference to: the quality of school self-evaluation; progress on achieving priorities in the school's improvement plan; impact of the support package; key competence issues and issues for celebration; and recommendations for the next phase of improvement.

Occasionally the situation within a school was such that it was felt necessary to establish an 'accelerated improvement board', to be convened and chaired by the headteacher. The other members of this board were the chair of governors, a representative of the local authority, a headteacher from a local cluster school and the Challenge Adviser. The main task of these boards, which would meet monthly, was to ensure that the improvement strategies were being implemented effectively and that rapid progress was being made.

Teamwork

Our earlier research underlined the importance of Challenge Advisers operating as a team (Ainscow and Howes, 2007). With this in mind, the Challenge teams met together on a regular basis.

While the content of the meetings varied, there were usually two core agenda items: first, a briefing regarding overall developments, including updates of policy changes from central government; and second, what was called the 'professional hour', during which members of the team debated the challenges they faced generally, and with regard to particular schools or local authorities. These discussions proved to be tremendous opportunities for collective learning, as these teams of highly experienced professionals argued about what actions should be taken. It was a privilege for me to sit back and reflect on the ideas that were generated.

In some instances, the challenges presented by certain schools meant they would occasionally be revisited during team meetings to hear about what progress, if any, was being made. For example, a primary school where overall standards were low in terms of attendance and results on national tests, and where there were concerns about poor behaviour among pupils, was a regular focus of attention. The school had seen a succession of headteachers, most of whom had stayed only for short periods. Meanwhile, confidence among staff had declined and there were regular disputes among staff and school governors, which led to the involvement of teacher unions.

Over a period of two years, the Challenge Adviser assigned to this particular school gradually came to grips with the situation, with support from other members of the team. Interestingly, I subsequently heard that the school had been graded 'outstanding' at an inspection.

Drawing lessons

In summary, an analysis of the work of the teams of Challenge Advisers in the two Challenge programmes suggests six important lessons.

1. *Start by analysing the context.* While there were some common factors that had previously prevented progress across the schools that were given intensive support, each one had to be analysed in detail.

2. *Mobilise leadership within the school.* In many cases, Advisers were able to identify other staff within the schools, including some

relatively inexperienced teachers and support staff, who had the potential to lead improvement efforts.

3. *Raise expectations.* Across the schools, the progress made led to changes in what staff members thought was possible.

4. *Connect to relevant external support.* A feature of schools that face challenging circumstances is that they tend to become isolated and inward-looking. With this in mind, advisers placed considerable emphasis on linking schools.

5. *Inject pace.* Moving forward with urgency was a central emphasis. The approach taken by the advisers was vital in this respect.

6. *Improve the image of the school within its community and more widely.* Within a context where schools are, to varying degrees, in competition with one another, external image is a vital factor.

In working with the teams of Challenge Advisers in Greater Manchester and Wales, I also occasionally asked them to reflect on two questions following their school visits.

1. *Did I make a difference to the school's effectiveness through my visit, or did I merely distract and disturb?* Always leave the school feeling better and more energised as the result of a visit. This emphatically doesn't mean becoming an 'uncritical friend' but using challenge and support in the best professional sense.

2. *What more should I do?* The acid test for any adviser is always to deliver promptly on any promises made during a visit.

Conclusion

While increased collaboration of the sort mentioned in this chapter is vital as a strategy for promoting equity, the experience of the two Challenge projects shows that it is not enough. The essential additional ingredient is an engagement with evidence that can bring an element of mutual challenge to such collaborative processes.

We found that evidence was particularly essential when linking schools, since collaboration is at its most powerful where partner schools are carefully matched and know what they are trying to achieve. Evidence also matters so schools go beyond cosy relationships that have no impact on outcomes. Consequently, schools need to base their relationships on evidence about each other's strengths and weaknesses so they can challenge each other to improve.

References

Ainscow, M (2015) *Towards Self-improving School Systems: Lessons from a City Challenge*. London: Routledge.

Ainscow, M, Chapman, C and Hadfield, M (2020) *Changing Education Systems: A Research-based Approach*. London: Routledge.

Ainscow, M and Howes, A (2007) Working Together to Improve Urban Secondary Schools: A Study of Practice in One City. *School Leadership and Management* 27(3): 285–300.

14 Weaving the ordinary magic of collaborative school improvement

DR KATE CHHATWAL, OBE

Key learning

- Education advisers can magnify their impact by harnessing and empowering school leaders to robustly evaluate practice and act on their findings.

- 'Done with' is better than 'done to', giving schools agency and insight to catalyse their improvement.

- Being part of something bigger multiplies opportunities for learning and system-wide growth.

AoEA criteria

- Criterion 6: Working in concert with the school's leadership

- Criterion 10: Providing critical evaluation of the quality of leadership

- Criterion 11: Providing critical evaluation of the quality of teaching

Introduction

I have always thought there is something magical about the conversations you hear in staffrooms – those moments when teachers and teaching assistants trade pedagogical approaches and the achievements of pupils in their care. Often these discussions focus on children facing additional challenges, whether special educational needs, difficult home circumstances or any of the myriad of other problems young people face. This is the ordinary magic of schools, the weft and warp of their craft.

The professional dialogue I overhear when I join a quality assurance review has similarly incredible properties and lies at the heart of

Challenge Partners' trademark approach to school evaluation and improvement, conducted in concert with each school's leadership. This chapter describes how reciprocity and collaboration combine to enable robust, improvement-inspiring evaluation of leadership and teaching through an annual drumbeat of peer review and support.

Our origin story: the London Challenge and Challenge Partners

Challenge Partners is a national practitioner-led education charity accelerating school improvement, leadership development and pupil progress. We share excellent practice across schools and trusts through rigorous peer reviews, tailored school improvement programmes, and national and local collaboration.

Our origins lie in a rich history of school improvement and collaboration, not least in the work of the London Challenge programme, launched by the UK Labour Government in 2003. The London Challenge's pioneering collaborative approach to school improvement included models of school-to-school support that unlocked great practice from schools and shared knowledge and practice between schools and local authorities.

When the London Challenge ended in 2011, some of the school leaders involved committed to developing a self-funding and sustainable way to continue and develop this approach nationally. Challenge Partners was born.

Thirteen years later, Challenge Partners is a thriving network of over 575 schools and 150 school trusts serving over 385,000 students. We welcome schools of all types, and our partnership encompasses primary, secondary, special and alternative provision schools; local authority maintained, academy, free school, grammar and independent schools; schools of all faiths and those of none. All are united by a commitment to collaboration and challenge to ensure great practice is not trapped in individual schools and that all young people can benefit.

The Challenge Partners' approach to school improvement

Challenge Partners' systemic approach to school improvement on a national scale is predicated on five defining characteristics:

1. *Being practitioner led.* Challenge Partners was founded by headteachers and practitioner leadership is integral to our governance and operations. This ensures our activities reflect, shape and respond to the real needs of teachers and leaders.

2. *A national network of local and regional partnerships.* Recognising the importance of place, Challenge Partners strengthens and harnesses local partnerships and regional collaboration, and provides funds to meet locally defined needs. These local and regional partnerships are united in a national Network of Excellence to tackle regional disparities and create a model and voice for national reform.

3. *Creating sustainable solutions.* We know there are no quick fixes. Our partnership supports schools and trusts in the long haul of deep and sustainable school improvement. We focus on the things that make the biggest difference: curriculum and pedagogy; leadership at all levels; and support for the pupils who need it most.

4. *Improving and sharing leading practice.* We systematically identify, credit and spread excellent practice to reduce variability within and between schools. By growing the top, we push the boundaries of exceptional performance, creating the capacity and knowledge to enable the whole system to move up. More poorly performing schools are supported to improve at the fastest rate, achieving what founding CEO Professor Sir George Berwick called 'upwards convergence' (Figure 14.1).

5. *Accessing the best from business and beyond.* We harness strong business and international models where they can stretch our schools and trust, recognising that we have much to learn from other sectors and jurisdictions.

Upwards convergence

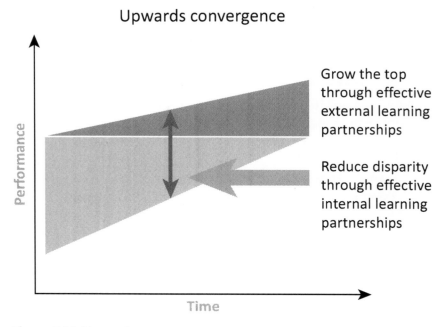

Figure 14.1: Upwards convergence

Our approach enables us to work towards our mission of reducing educational inequality and improving the life chances of all children. Schools and trusts in our partnership have collectively adopted three aims:

1. to maximise the life chances of all pupils and accelerate the progress of the disadvantaged;

2. to support leaders at all levels to develop and grow capacity for sustained improvement in schools and trusts; and

3. to extend excellence, shaping a world-class system in which all pupils thrive.

Progress against these aims is the way we assess our impact.

Quality Assurance Review: the comma in an ongoing school improvement dialogue

The Quality Assurance Review (QAR) is the beating heart of Challenge Partners' approach to individual school improvement and systemic upwards convergence. Since 2011, almost 6000 school leaders have been trained as peer reviewers, reviewing well over 3000 schools between them. In 2023/24, a record 475 schools from the Isles of Scilly to Sunderland will host a QAR and reciprocate by sending their Challenge Partners' trained headteachers and senior leaders to review other schools in the network, providing continuous professional development for all leaders involved.

Guided by an expert Lead Reviewer, external peer reviewers work in tandem with the host school's leaders to evaluate the school's performance in pedagogy, curriculum and leadership at all levels. All review activities are conducted jointly, and all outputs are agreed with the school. We refer to this as 'one team, two parts', and it is crucial to ensuring that the QAR is 'done with, not to' the school being reviewed (a philosophy we were using long before Ofsted adopted the term). It is during the scheduled time after each activity, when the internal and external leaders discuss and evaluate what they have seen using rubric and tools developed by Challenge Partners, that the ordinary magic of rich professional dialogue and learning about core strategies and practice occurs.

The schools that benefit most are those that make themselves vulnerable, sharing the things they are finding hard, not just what is going well. The carefully designed process and ethos embolden them to do this by drawing external reviewers from beyond the locality and assuring confidentiality throughout. The host school leaders' involvement in all review activities means they can see for themselves the evidence being gathered and capture key learnings and actions in their own notes. The final report, summarising 'what went well' and agreed 'even better if' provides an aide memoire and record for governors but can never replicate the deep insights gathered through active participation in the review. The report is confidential to the school being reviewed and the school decides who to share it with. Schools are also able to decide whether they wish it to include 'peer evaluation estimates' of their performance on a three-point scale, where 'leading' refers to exceptional practice and recognises the school's impact on raising the quality of education in other schools.

The review and report focus on the core business of schools: curriculum, pedagogy and leadership at all levels. Since 2019, QARs have included a sharper focus than ever on the quality of provision and outcomes for pupils from under-resourced backgrounds and/ or with additional needs. The themes are explored through activities shaped by what each school hopes to gain from the review and based on methodologies specified in our training and handbooks. Core activities include: meetings to explore strategy and impact, and quality of provision and outcomes; paired learning explorations; and meetings/interviews with middle leaders, staff, pupils and governors.

Lead Reviewers play a crucial role in upholding the rigour and ethos of the review process. They work with the host school to agree the review programme, including any specific focus and tenor. They ensure that evidence is captured and evaluated with accuracy and rigour, and write the final report. They also provide coaching for all the participating leaders, making it a valuable CPD experience.

Lead Reviewers are recruited by Challenge Partners for their substantial school evaluation and improvement experience, which often includes inspectorial work. The demanding selection, training and onboarding process ensures our Lead Reviewers embody Challenge Partners' ethos as well as the necessary skills. Once appointed, they receive biannual training and regular quality assurance of their work. To ensure consistency and high standards, every QAR report is scrutinised by a 'QA Reader' before being shared with the school.

We describe the QAR as a comma in an ongoing school improvement dialogue. The annual peer audit punctuates the school's annual cycle of evaluation, planning and action. It helps schools to determine where they are, where they want to get to and what they need to do next. The 'how' depends on work beyond the review, supported by schools in the local hub and national Network of Excellence. Together, they share expertise through structured 'knowledge-exchange' activities and engage in joint practice development. At a time when teachers and funds are in short supply, pooling resources and not having to reinvent wheels have never been so valuable to schools. They also benefit from exposure to speakers and ideas from other sectors and jurisdictions to expand their horizons and explore the art of the possible.

Impact: multiple gains

In an independent evaluation by Dr Peter Matthews and Marcia Headon, the QAR was found to deliver multiple gains. It benefits schools with their evaluation and improvement, and peer reviewers with professional development and ideas and contacts to take back to their own settings. It also enables systemic improvement and upwards convergence by finding excellent and promising practice – accredited through the review process – to spread through the partnership and beyond using Challenge Partners' established knowledge exchange methodologies.

The external challenge provided in QARs mitigates the risks of relying only on internal reviews and guards against stagnation and group think. Bringing in outside perspectives extends and refreshes thinking among school and trust leaders. This is achieved both by inviting peer practitioners in and reciprocally sending leaders out to evaluate and learn from practice elsewhere. The breadth and diversity of our partnership allows participants to draw from many different approaches and contexts.

Like every Challenge Partners' programme and network, the QAR builds in unique professional development for middle, senior and executive leaders. This isn't CPD in a training room; it is rich experiential learning under the guidance of Lead Reviewers and facilitators whose skill in coaching ensures every development opportunity is seized. Many schools tell us that participation in Challenge Partners is as central to their CPD strategy as it is to their school improvement strategy.

Analysis of public examinations data at Key Stage 2 and Key Stage 4 reveals consistently how schools in Challenge Partners outperform the national average, despite serving a high proportion of disadvantaged pupils. Inspection data also confirms that schools that look up and out – that are open to challenge, collaboration and new ideas – perform better. It is striking how schools in our network were more likely to achieve or sustain an 'outstanding' inspection grade or move from 'inadequate' or 'requires improvement' to at least 'good'. While we cannot establish direct causation, it is clear that something in the discipline of annual audit and hard-edged collaboration serves Challenge Partners' schools well.

Conclusion

The important job of school improvement needn't be a solo endeavour, either for Education Advisers or school leadership teams. In networks like Challenge Partners, they have a chance to come together, pooling resources and expertise to make the task easier, more impactful and even more enjoyable. Their collaboration should be hard-edged, demanding high standards of rigour and evidence to inform evaluation and action, harnessing and amplifying the ordinary magic of practitioner insight and dialogue.

 Further reading

Chhatwal, K (2021) It's All About Trust! Developing Trust Leaders. *Teaching Times*. [online]. Available at: www.teachingtimes.com/its-all-about-trust-developing-trust-leaders-and-improving-school-trusts (accessed 30 June 2024).

Matthews, P and Headon, M (2015) *Multiple Gains. An Independent Evaluation of Challenge Partners' Peer Reviews of Schools.* London: Institute of Education Press.

NAHT (2019) *The Principle of Effective School-to-School Peer Review.* London: Haywards Heath.

15 Schools North East: a case study in regional collaboration

CHRIS ZARRAGA

Key learning

- No two regions are the same.

- A single representative voice for all headteachers from across the region has assisted in the regional challenges being better understood by policy-makers and educationalists nationally.

- To be truly collaborative and representative of the region's needs, all the organisation's activity has to be focused on the schools' identified priorities, school-led and/or co-constructed with school leaders.

- A regional voice and collaborative organisation of schools spanning all sectors has helped to provide both the professional support network and collective resolve, resilience and expertise to continuously improve together.

AoEA criteria

- Criterion 6: Working in concert with the school's leadership

- Criterion 8: Understanding of causal factors impacting on school performance

- Criterion 14: Having an up-to-date knowledge of relevant educational policy, inspection and other related issues

Introduction

At Schools North East, we are no strangers to regional collaboration. In fact, we would go as far as to say that we are pioneers of it.

We are the first (and only!) schools-led regional network in the United Kingdom. As a charity, we represent all 1150 schools across all 12 local authorities in the North East region, and we have been on quite a journey.

The roots of the organisation can be found in the belief of Les Walton CBE and a small group of headteachers keen to ensure that school leaders had a voice nationally that the challenges facing the education sector across the North East needed to be more fully understood and that in turn this might better inform national policy. Now we've reached heights we once didn't think were possible.

As with the National Network of Special Schools (NNoSS) for School Business Professionals, our work is now recognised nationally too. NNoSS represents all special and hospital schools, and alternative provisions right across England.

Forming an alliance and building deep-rooted relationships with our region's CEOs, headteachers, deputy headteachers, school business professionals and teachers means Schools North East is able to be many things:

- *The voice*. We put a strong regional accent on the education debate, injecting the national conversation with local concerns to guarantee the right support.
- *The glue*. We help the community to stay connected while encouraging new and existing relationships to flourish.
- *The bridge*. We are the bridge between our region's schools and politicians, policy-makers, universities, think tanks, and funding organisations that operate beyond our region's borders.

The power of collaboration

Everything we do is a result of collaboration, from our successful calendar of annual events to in-depth interviews with regional and national media on our schools' most critical issues. Without the co-operation and collaborative power of North East schools, there is no Schools North East.

Regional collaboration was the foundation on which the organisation was built, after a region-wide consultation in 2007 revealed that North East schools desperately needed support in getting their voices heard. After realising that the region's schools were constantly left out of the education debate, we concluded that 'enough is enough'.

We knew the North East needed and warranted being at the front and centre of these crucial discussions. The vision was that, through effective collaboration, our school colleagues and young people would flourish – but only within well-resourced, nurturing, and purposeful school environments.

So Schools North East was born, as a grassroots organisation to encourage the positive, long-lasting change that our region's schools so desperately needed. From the outset, it was mutually understood that the power of collaboration could maximise outcomes and increase potential – not only for North East students, but for all education staff. And, by watering both plants in equal measure, the entire region blossoms.

Seventeen years later, the organisation is stronger than ever, having transitioned from a whisper in 2007 to a roar in 2024. Through teamwork, determination and a genuine belief that together we can craft a better system for students and staff to thrive, the organisation has been catapulted to heights that were once upon a time thought impossible.

What this collaboration looks like

By working together as a region, we constantly highlight the wide disconnect between our region's schools and policy-makers, but we don't stop there. Our team also lobbies for the relevant solutions and changes to ensure that this detachment doesn't harm the operation and outcomes of our schools.

We strongly believe that education policies should never be approached as a one-size-fits-all process; no two regions are the same, so why would our strategies be the same? While it is important to note that things have progressed positively and significantly since 2007, the fact remains that policies for North East schools tend to be made by people who live a long, long way from here. At Schools North East, we speak openly and often about the vast disparities between our region and some others, and ask how it makes sense to enforce the exact same strategies in Gateshead as we do, for example, in Greenwich.

If we continue to standardise policy, we risk a continuing widening of the gap between the North East and other, often more affluent, regions. Recognition of the perennial contextual challenges is a must, which is exactly what Schools North East does in collaboration with the wider education community. Once we know what the most common pressing issues are, we can then begin advocating for better solutions.

State of the Region survey

Our State of the Region survey is just one example of how we collaborate to dig deeper into our schools' concerns and challenges – not those of schools in London, or Cornwall, or another part of the country, which may have completely different issues, motivations and challenges, but those of the North East.

Each term, we circulate a survey to better understand how education staff are currently coping with different key areas such as attendance, well-being, and recruitment and retention. While it serves many purposes, the main driving force behind this survey is to explore and highlight some of the real issues our pupils and colleagues face, so we know exactly what policy-makers should be focusing on.

Policy direction, we believe, is too infrequently aligned to what those on the frontline are saying is needed most. For example, are initiatives such as 'Maths to 18' or introducing a new qualification post-age 16 providing real answers to what is needed in the North East – or elsewhere for that matter? What we are given isn't always necessarily what we need, so collaboration with our region's schools allows us to identify the priorities most pertinent to them as a counter-balance so we can engage with decision-makers in a more informed way.

The results of this synergy

Our engagement with our school community continues to reach new heights, year on year. Each year, around 4000 colleagues participate in our events and professional learning programme.

The voice of our schools has become more prominent year on year. We are regularly approached with requests from radio, print and TV for the North East perspective on a vast range of topics, including GCSEs, A-levels, the state of our school buildings, the disadvantaged gap, long-term deprivation and attendance, to name but a few.

Just a few years ago, at our annual leadership summit, the then Chief Inspector of Schools in England was heavily critical of our secondary schools and our school leaders, declaring that they were the reason why the North East was behind the South in key performance measures.

Fast forward to 2023 and all the summer GCSE and A Level results media coverage was focused entirely on the impact of long-term disadvantage, the COVID-19 pandemic and the ongoing cost-of-living crisis on our children, schools and results. There was nothing about this being the fault of our schools – and rightly so! Even the Minister of State for Schools in August 2023 stated that the issue facing North East education was long-term deprivation, not the quality of our schools. Sensibly, this is no longer part of the narrative.

The need for sustained, regional collaboration

There has never been a greater need for collaboration among North East schools. The impact of the cost-of-living crisis, combined with the pandemic, has left wounds too deep to cover with a plaster.

Schools will continue to need Schools North East – and vice versa – for as long as the education system exists. Each new policy, election, problem and trend will be given due attention and our organisation will be there as the representative voice for the North East's schools and their families.

At the heart of all our efforts sits the Schools North East manifesto, which underpins our work. Created with our partner schools, it is the main platform we use to focus on influencing the development of education policy regionally and nationally, and we are constantly revisiting this document to ensure its current accuracy and relevance.

It is clear from our ongoing data analysis and research that the North East faces some quite unique challenges. Schools North East has a key role to play helping to ensure that these challenges are understood and that they inform both regional and national policy, as advocated in our manifesto and summarised as follows.

- *Recognise the regional context.* Education policy that supports positive outcomes for the North East's pupils must take into account the context in which it is implemented. The effectiveness of one policy may be different in areas with different challenges.

- *Promote a positive narrative around North East education.* Schools and teachers face increasing pressures. We must not forget the many successes of our schools and avoid fixating on failure. While we cannot be naïve about the challenges they face, we must rightly celebrate the hard work, professionalism and expertise of our leaders and teachers.

- *Depoliticise education.* So long as education is treated as a 'political football', the different contexts in which our schools work won't get the attention needed. In the development of education policy, standards and practices must be adopted that create effective legislation and practice that will support the region's needs.

- *Evidence-based policy-making.* To depoliticise education and ensure the above principles are incorporated, education policy must be evidence based. The voice of the teaching profession must be 'front and centre' in this. Practitioner experience must not be sidelined and needs to involve wider consultation at the 'chalkface' and a more considered pace of change and long-term planning.

- *A long-term view.* Constant changes to policy and practice serve only to frustrate school leaders, drive good people from the profession, waste public money and prevent proper evaluation and assessment of whether policies are succeeding.

- *Greater support for early years.* An education policy that takes the context into account and is evidence-based requires targeted policy and funding. Greater support for early years is crucial for tackling the disadvantage gap in attainment.

- *A joined-up approach from cabinet to the chalkface.* Policy changes must be considered in the light of all other education policies and initiatives, and policies spanning other government departments. The 'law of unintended consequences' because of a lack of joined-up policy must be minimised wherever possible.

- *Support the North East's teaching profession at every level.* Attracting teachers to disadvantaged areas isn't simply a matter of financial incentive. Our teaching staff should have clear continuous professional learning relevant to their context and benefit from a culture where progression is typical. Teacher workload and stress must be addressed, with better access to well-being services.

- *Ensure all pupils can access an appropriate curriculum.* The current national curriculum allows a great deal of flexibility, and this needs to be maintained, encouraging local learning opportunities. However, despite this degree of flexibility, not all schools and pupils can access the same quality of entitlement.

- *Targeted support for those with the greatest needs.* Funding and resources must target the region's areas of greatest need with the ambition of making the support they receive the envy of the world.

Conclusion

Fostering a collaborative spirit among educators in the North East isn't just 'nice to have'; it is a key driver of progress.

By sharing expertise, innovating together and supporting one another, educators can refine their craft, improve student outcomes and ultimately create a more effective and enriching learning environment for everyone.

However, schools cannot do it alone. They are not an island, and overcoming challenge requires a joined-up approach between the services and agencies that support children and young people. Increasingly, schools feel as if they are having to shoulder these burdens alone, insufficiently supported by national policy and, as a consequence, wider support services.

To ensure that schools' needs across the region are understood and that the formulation and impact of policy is well informed, Schools North East will continue to provide a strong and representative voice for its headteachers in striving for the best possible education and life chances for its children and young people.

 Further reading

Schools North East (2019) *Manifesto for North East Education.* Available at: https://schoolsnortheast.org (accessed 5 May 2024).

16 Fostering collaboration and capacity-building in the nursery sector

CLARE EVANS

Key learning

- Post-lockdown effects on young children require innovative collaboration at the nursery leadership level.

- Identifying specific areas of developmental delay through data collection is crucial.

- Establishing dissolvable clusters and resource hubs fosters effective knowledge-sharing and support.

- Collaborative training and support empower schools to address children's emotional and developmental needs, based on six nurture principles and trauma-informed practice.

AoEA criteria

- Criterion 6: Working in concert with the school's leadership

- Criterion 8: Understanding of causal factors impacting on school performance

- Criterion 9: Providing critical evaluation of performance

- Criterion 10: Providing critical evaluation of the quality of leadership

- Criterion 12: Providing critical evaluation of pastoral provision

- Criterion 13: Providing critical evaluation of collaborative working between governors, leaders and staff

- Criterion 14: Having an up-to-date knowledge of relevant educational policy and other related issues

Introduction

The COVID-19 pandemic presented unprecedented challenges for the early years education sector in Northern Ireland. As the world emerged from lockdowns, it became increasingly evident that significant learning losses had occurred, disproportionately impacting our most vulnerable students. The disruptions caused by the pandemic rippled through the sector, leaving both students and educators reeling from its effects. As the Chair of the Area Learning Community in West Belfast, a collective of 26 nursery schools, I recognised the critical importance of addressing these challenges head-on and empowering our colleagues to meet the diverse needs of their students effectively. The path forward required a collaborative effort and strategic change management approach.

Identifying the challenges

Professor Barry Carpenter of Ofsted identified five key losses experienced by children during the lockdowns: routine, structure, friendship, opportunity and freedom (2020). These losses manifested in children entering nursery and school settings far from ready to learn, posing a significant hurdle for our early years professionals. During a series of meetings with representatives from each nursery, I listened intently to the concerns voiced by our frontline staff. It became apparent that in addition to the five losses identified for children, our educators were grappling with their own set of losses, leaving them feeling ill-equipped to support their students effectively.

The five losses experienced by staff during lockdowns had a profound impact on their confidence and ability to effectively support their students' learning and development.

1. *Loss of learning momentum.* As the natural flow of instruction was disrupted, educators struggled with how to pick up where they left off and accelerate progress. This loss of momentum shook their confidence in their ability to close widening achievement gaps.

2. *Loss of social and emotional development opportunities.* Without the in-person classroom setting, it became enormously challenging

for staff to foster the social-emotional skills that are so critical during the early years. Many felt they were not equipped to nurture this area of development virtually.

3. *Loss of routine and structure.* The lack of established routines and schedules left staff floundering to create stability. This loss of structure was disorienting and detrimental to their instructional abilities, given that young students thrive on predictable patterns.

4. *Loss of access to resources.* The sudden remote learning transition exposed disparities in access to learning materials, both digital and physical. Educators felt hamstrung in their ability to provide quality instruction without sufficient resources at their fingertips.

5. *Loss of staff confidence and morale.* Most critically, the stresses of lockdown and the transition to virtual learning left many early years professionals overwhelmed, anxious and lacking confidence in their skills. This drastic loss of morale severely undermined their ability to perform their roles effectively.

As they prepared to welcome students back in person, this convergence of losses had depleted staff's sense of self-efficacy. Many questioned whether they could re-engage students, accelerate academic progress and attend to social-emotional needs after such significant disruption. Rebuilding their confidence was pivotal to empower educators and ensure that they could meet the diverse needs of their incoming students.

Implementing change management

To address these challenges, we conducted a force field analysis as described by psychologist Kurt Lewin (1951). This involved identifying the driving forces for change, such as the need to address learning losses and support children's well-being, as well as potential restraining forces, such as staff anxiety and resource constraints. By understanding these forces, we would develop strategies to strengthen the drivers and mitigate the restraints.

We then implemented a Kaizen approach of continuous improvement (Imai, 1986). This involved setting up a virtual team site as a hub for communication, resource-sharing and professional development. Staff could connect, exchange ideas and learn from one another's experiences. We also implemented questionnaires and polls to gather ongoing feedback and ensure our efforts remained relevant and responsive.

One area where collective capacity-building had been notably absent was in fostering a sense of community and shared expertise among the nursery sector professionals. While individual nurseries had their strengths and strategies, there was a lack of a cohesive platform for knowledge-sharing and collaborative problem-solving. This gap presented an opportunity to build a more connected and resilient network within our sector.

To bridge this divide, I initiated the development of a virtual team site, which served as a hub for communication, resource-sharing and professional development. This platform allowed staff from different nursery clusters to connect, exchange ideas and learn from one another's experiences. By fostering an environment of open dialogue and collaboration, we aimed to leverage the collective knowledge and expertise within our community.

Additionally, we implemented a series of questionnaires and polls on the team site, enabling staff to voice their concerns, share their successes and provide feedback on the initiatives being implemented. This two-way communication ensured that our efforts remained relevant and responsive to the evolving needs of our colleagues and students. By actively involving our frontline educators in the decision-making process, we cultivated a sense of ownership and empowerment within the community.

Building sector knowledge and expertise

Recognising the importance of building sector knowledge and expertise, I organised targeted training sessions and workshops tailored to address the five losses of lockdown. These sessions covered a wide range of topics, including emotional literacy activities, fostering peer interactions, establishing consistent routines, and effective utilisation of digital and physical resources.

One particularly impactful session focused on supporting the social and emotional development of our young learners. Facilitated by a renowned expert in the field, this workshop provided practical strategies for creating nurturing classroom environments that fostered emotional intelligence and healthy peer interactions. Participants left with a comprehensive toolkit of activities and techniques to implement in their classrooms, empowering them to address this critical area of development effectively.

Furthermore, we facilitated regular coaching sessions and team-building activities, fostering a supportive and collaborative environment. These initiatives not only provided practical strategies but also helped to rebuild staff confidence and morale, which had been significantly impacted by the disruptions caused by the lockdowns.

One particularly powerful exercise involved small group discussions where educators shared their individual experiences and challenges during the pandemic. This open and honest dialogue allowed for a deeper understanding of the emotional toll the lockdowns had taken on our staff. It also created a safe space for vulnerability and connection, reminding our colleagues that they were not alone in their struggles.

Regular Plan-Do-Study-Act (PDSA) cycles allowed us to rapidly test and refine our interventions. For example, when a training session on creating nurturing classroom environments received positive feedback, we quickly rolled it out to more clusters and incorporated key learnings into our resource library.

Celebrating successes

Throughout the process, we made a concerted effort to celebrate successes and recognise the challenging work of our early years professionals. Their unwavering commitment to their students' well-being and academic progress was truly inspiring, and it was my privilege to support them in this important work. Regular recognition and appreciation events, both virtual and in-person, helped to boost morale and foster a sense of pride within our community. This positive reinforcement was a key driver for sustaining momentum.

Results and continuous improvement

The results of our change-management approach and capacity-building efforts were far reaching. By addressing the five losses of lockdown systematically and collaboratively, we witnessed a marked improvement in student engagement, academic progress and overall well-being. I was able to pull together our work and create a toolkit, which was shared across our Area Learning Community. Staff regained confidence and felt empowered to tackle challenges head on, armed with the necessary knowledge, resources and support.

One particularly inspiring success story involved a nursery school that had been severely impacted on by the loss of routine and structure during the lockdowns. Staff were off on long-term sick leave, and morale was at rock bottom. Through the implementation of consistent schedules, visual aids and clear expectations, the educators in this school were able to create a sense of predictability and security for their students. This, in turn, facilitated a smoother transition back to in-person learning and helped to mitigate the potential negative impact on academic and social development, and harmonise staffing.

Moving forward, our Area Learning Community remains committed to continuous improvement and professional development. The lessons learned during this process have reinforced the importance of proactive planning, open communication and a shared commitment to meeting the diverse needs of our students and staff.

A mentorship program was established to provide guidance to new educators and foster knowledge-sharing. Our expanded virtual team site includes a comprehensive resource library to enable ongoing learning. These initiatives serve to sustain the momentum of our capacity-building efforts and ensure that our community continues to grow and adapt in the face of future challenges.

Conclusion

The capacity-building journey demonstrated the power of collective effort and strategic change management in addressing pressing community needs. By conducting a force field analysis, implementing Kaizen continuous improvement and empowering educators, we built a stronger, more resilient nursery sector better equipped to support the holistic development of our youngest learners.

Our success serves as a reminder that even in the face of unprecedented challenges, dedicated professionals can come together to create positive change and ensure that every child can thrive. By fostering a culture of collaboration, sharing knowledge and empowering our educators, we have built a stronger and more resilient nursery sector in Northern Ireland, better equipped to navigate future challenges, and support the holistic development of our youngest learners. Our success serves as a model for creating positive change in the face of adversity.

 Further reading

The following resources should provide valuable additional insights and practical strategies to support the ongoing work of fostering collaboration, building capacity and supporting the well-being of young children and early years professionals in the post-pandemic era.

Bridges, W (1991) *Managing Transitions: Making the Most of Change*. Reading, MA: Addison-Wesley.

Carpenter, B and Carpenter, M (2020) A Recovery Curriculum: Loss and Life for our Children and Schools Post Pandemic. Available at: www.ssatuk.co.uk/blog/a-recovery-curriculum-loss-and-life-for-our-children-and-schools-post-pandemic (accessed 30 June 2024). This article delves deeper into the concept of the 'five losses' and proposes a recovery curriculum to help schools support students post-lockdown.

$\longrightarrow$

Craig, S E (2016) *Trauma-Sensitive Schools: Learning Communities Transforming Children's Lives', K–5*. New York: Teachers College Press. This book provides a framework for creating trauma-sensitive schools and offers practical strategies for supporting students who have experienced adversity, which is particularly relevant in the context of the pandemic.

Davis, G and Ryder, G (2019) *Leading in Early Childhood*. Thousand Oaks, CA: Sage. While not specifically focused on the pandemic, this book offers valuable insights into effective leadership practices in the early years sector, including strategies for fostering collaboration and professional development.

Deming, W E (1986) *Out of the Crisis*. Cambridge, MA: MIT Press.

DuFour, R and Reason, C (2016) *Professional Learning Communities at Work and Virtual Collaboration: On the Tipping Point of Transformation*. Bloomington, IN: Solution Tree. This book explores the power of professional learning communities and how virtual collaboration can enhance their impact, which aligns with the strategies discussed in the chapter.

Heath, C and Heath, D (2010) *Switch: How to Change Things When Change is Hard*. New York: Broadway Books.

Hiatt, J (2006) *ADKAR: A Model for Change in Business, Government, and Our Community*. Loveland, CO: Prosci Learning Center Publications.

Kibble, K and Bryce-Clegg, A (2021) *The Six Principles of Nurture: A Framework for Supporting Social and Emotional Development in Early Childhood*. London: Nurture UK. This book delves into the six nurture principles mentioned in the key learnings and provides guidance on how to apply them in early childhood settings.

Kotter, J P (1996) *Leading Change*. Boston: Harvard Business School Press.

Rodd, J (2021) *Leadership in Early Childhood: The Pathway to Professionalism*. London: Routledge. This book offers a comprehensive overview of leadership in the early years sector, including strategies for building professional capacity and fostering a culture of continuous improvement.

Rogers, E M (1962) *Diffusion of Innovations*. New York: Free Press.

Senge, P M (1990) *The Fifth Discipline: The Art and Practice of the Learning Organisation*. New York: Doubleday.

 References

Carpenter, B (2020) *Statement on the 5 Losses of Lockdown for Children*. London: Ofsted.

Imai, M (1986) *Kaizen: The Key to Japan's Competitive Success*. New York: McGraw-Hill.

Lewin, K (1951) *Field Theory in Social Science*. New York: Harper & Row.

Conclusions: reflections on Book 2, *Advising on School Improvement*

DR TONY BIRCH, IAN LANE AND LES WALTON, CBE

In pursuit of educational excellence, the role of the School Improvement Adviser (SIA) is pivotal. Tasked with fostering positive change and sustaining a focus on continuous improvement across an educational landscape, SIAs play a crucial role that requires a blend of expertise, insightful analysis and the ability to foster and enable collaboration. From working in concert with school leadership teams to critically evaluating various facets of educational provision, their contributions can be hugely instrumental in shaping the trajectory of student success. In this second book in The Education Adviser series, we have delved into the intricacies of the SIA's role, highlighting its significance and impact on educational advancement. Professor David Hopkins' Chapter 7 on 'unleashing greatness' exemplifies the scope of this.

Working in concert with the school's leadership

As illustrated in our first book, at the heart of the SIA's role lies the ability to apply a unique skillset in asserting professional credibility, building trust and working effectively with the school's leadership. This improvement partnership serves as the cornerstone for initiating transformative changes and driving continuous improvement. By forging strong and insightful working relationships with school leaders, SIAs facilitate the alignment of a strategic vision, goals and actions; Chapter 11 by Ian Lane illustrates this particularly well. Through open channels of communication and shared decision-making processes, they harness collective expertise to navigate challenges and maximise opportunity. Chapter 4 by Stuart Adlam illustrates this through the example of supporting new headteachers. By fostering a culture of collaboration and mutual respect, SIAs empower school leaders to lead with confidence and agility, thus fostering an environment conducive to innovation, growth and continuous improvement: this ethic is at the heart of Chapter 13 by Professor Mel Ainscow, CBE and Chapter 14 by Dr Kate Chhatwal, OBE.

Insightful and well-written reports

One of the hallmarks of an adept SIA is their ability to produce and talk to clear, insightful and well-written reports that provide valuable guidance for both school leaders and governors. These reports often serve as a catalyst for change, offering a comprehensive analysis of the current state of affairs while pinpointing areas for further improvement. Through the collaborative and meticulous examination of performance data, assessment outcomes and inspection findings, SIAs unearth valuable insights that help to inform strategic decision-making and intervention strategies. In their reporting, they challenge underperformance and offer recommendations tailored to the unique needs of each school community they serve. On a larger scale Chris Zarraga's Chapter 15 shows the powerful influence of communication in his account of the impact of Schools North East.

Understanding causal factors

A distinguishing trait of effective SIAs is their ability to delve deeply into the causal factors contributing to a school's performance. Armed with analytical prowess and diagnostic skills, they unravel the complex interplay of internal and external factors shaping educational outcomes. This is detailed effectively in Tom Grieveson's Chapter 2. By conducting thorough causal analyses, SIAs uncover underlying issues and systemic challenges that impede progress. This nuanced understanding enables them, as Rebecca Jackson exemplifies in Chapter 3, to tailor interventions that address root causes rather than symptoms, thus fostering sustainable improvement over time. In Chapter 1, Les Walton provides another perspective through his reflections of connecting with context.

Analysis of all aspects of a school's performance

Central to the SIA's role is the insightful analysis of all aspects of a school's performance. From academic achievements to pastoral care provision, they leave no stone unturned in their quest to drive excellence. By scrutinising test and examination data, internal assessment information, inspection evidence and stakeholder voice, they paint a comprehensive picture of the school's strengths and areas for further development. In Chapter 16, Clare Evans illustrates how a sensitivity to context and drive for change can lead to impact for children. This holistic perspective enables leaders, governors and other key stakeholders to make informed decisions and allocate resources strategically, thus maximising the impact of actions. Kevan Naughton's account in Chapter 6 demonstrates how implementing the curriculum is a complex process requiring consideration of a range of factors.

Critical evaluation of leadership, teaching and pastoral provision

Critical evaluation forms the bedrock of the SIA's work, encompassing leadership, teaching and pastoral provision. With a discerning eye, they assess the quality of leadership and governance structures, evaluating the efficacy of self-evaluation protocols and the translation of analysis into targeted actions. Similarly, they assist in scrutinising pedagogical practice, curriculum design and assessment strategy to ensure alignment with student needs and educational objectives. In Chapter 12, Peter Parish shows how this can be turned into effective action through a school improvement plan. SIAs also assist in an evaluation of the effectiveness of pastoral support mechanisms to meet the diverse needs of students, with a view to fostering a nurturing and fully inclusive learning environment.

Critical and collective evaluation of outcomes

Building on the causal impact of educational provision, in their quest for excellence, SIAs critically evaluate how governors, leaders and staff collaborate to achieve improvement in student outcomes. By assessing the coherence and effectiveness of improvement strategies, they identify areas of synergy and potential areas for refinement – an approach that Narinder Gill exemplifies effectively in Chapter 10. Through constructive feedback and ongoing support, SIAs empower stakeholders to refine their approaches and embrace evidence-based practices that drive positive change.

Up-to-date knowledge

In a rapidly evolving educational landscape, staying abreast of the latest developments is imperative for SIAs. Chapter 8 by Emma Tarrant and Chapter 9 by Michaela Barber show the importance of this in continually developing teachers and leaders, and thus illustrate how advisers can use this effectively to support capacity-building. In contrast, in Chapter 5 Mairéad Mhig Uaid shows how an approach that is context specific can emerge as a powerful educational innovation. Armed with up-to-date knowledge of educational policy, inspection frameworks, legislative changes and emerging research, SIAs navigate complexities with confidence and agility. By synthesising diverse sources of information, they offer informed perspectives and innovative solutions that address contemporary challenges and opportunities.

Conclusion

In conclusion, the role of the SIA is a multifaceted one, which is unique in nurturing and enabling educational excellence with those leaders with whom the SIA works. Through collaborative, insightful analysis and critical evaluation, SIAs assist in empowering school communities to embark on a journey of continuous improvement and innovation. By harnessing collective expertise and fostering a culture of learning and reflection, they pave the way for a brighter future, where every student has the opportunity to thrive and succeed. The chapters in *Advising on School Improvement* bring together and to life many examples of exemplary practice from specialists in their field and from across a range of jurisdictions.

The following table summarises the learning that this book brings together.

Criterion	Key learning	Chapters
6. Working in concert with the school's leadership	The adviser will make little if any sustainable difference unless they work in concert with leaders to support, challenge and enable effective change. The SIA will need to draw on the full range of advisory skills and professional expertise to assist leaders in developing their organisation. It is a skilful process, since all organisations and their leaders are very different.	1 2 3 4 5 6 7 8 9 10 11 12 13 14 15 16
7. Providing, clear, insightful and well-written reports	The adviser must understand the importance and influence of a well-written report. Challenge needs to be well-evidenced, clearly articulated and managed carefully, sensitive to the audience.	11 12 13
8. Understanding of causal factors impacting on school improvement	The SIA must understand the importance of and the critical link between cause and effect in the evaluation of a school's performance – what is contributing effectively to the progress that is being made and what might be holding the school back. Causation is the key to unlocking why a school or college is underperforming and in determining what then needs to be addressed.	1 2 3 5 6 7 8 10 11 12 13 15 16

Criterion	Key learning	Chapters
9. Providing critical evaluation of performance	Understanding the full range of evidence available to them in relation to a school's performance, and working with leaders, the SIA needs to be able to assess and evaluate where provision is strong and where it can be improved. Judgements need to be well evidenced, carefully and, where necessary, sensitively arrived at and given with a view to empowering leaders in addressing the next steps with their staff.	2 3 4 6 12 13 16
10. Providing critical evaluation of the quality of leadership	Working in concert with the school's leadership in providing a critical evaluation of the quality of leadership, inclusive of their own, is a skilful process and, when done well, will require a high degree of emotional intelligence, a good range of evidence inclusive of quality 360° feedback and impact on performance. The criteria for evaluating the quality of leadership and the range of evidence to be used will need to be clearly understood and agreed by both the commissioner of the advice and the adviser prior to the work being undertaken. Regulatory frameworks are often used for this type of advisory work, but these can arguably be limiting.	2 4 6 7 10 11 12 13 14 16
11. Providing critical evaluation of the quality of teaching	Agreement will need to be reached in relation to the criteria, frame of reference and scope of the evidence to be used in forming a view of the quality of teaching. Pupil voice is arguably critical, as is the quality of work produced by pupils recently, currently and over time. The link with and impact of the leadership of this area of provision will also be an important factor in evaluating the quality of the provision.	3 4 6 7 10 14

Criterion	Key learning	Chapters
12. Providing critical evaluation of pastoral provision	Again, agreement will need to be reached in relation to the criteria, frame of reference and scope of the evidence to be used in forming a view of the quality of pastoral provision. Pupil, staff and parental voices are arguably critical, as are behaviours for learning currently seen and evidenced over time. As with teaching, the link with the leadership of this area of provision will be an important factor in forming a view.	3 4 16
13. Providing critical evaluation of collaborative working between governors, leaders and staff.	The adviser has a key role to play in determining how effectively governors, leaders and staff work in concert with each other in providing the best possible education for their pupils. Clarity of role, delegated authority, purposeful meetings and a climate of mutual support, challenge and trust should characterise effective working.	1 2 4 7 10 11 12 13 16
14. Having an up-to-date knowledge of relevant educational policy, inspection and other related issues	SIAs must keep abreast of the most recent changes in educational policy, regulatory frameworks and their potential for impacting on the schools and settings they advise. Changes are also subject to variation across jurisdictions, so it is best to check.	1 2 5 6 7 8 9 10 11 12 13 15 16

As illustrated in both Books 1 and 2 in this series, the influence of and the difference made by education advisers as they seek to empower the leaders with whom they work in enabling effective change is not to be underestimated. The well thought-through and careful deployment of advisers will serve to assist any organisation that is striving to continuously improve, irrespective of their size, complexity or jurisdiction.

> *The vision of the AoEA is that every school, college and education provider has access to high quality support, advice and challenge, which is independent and focused on improving outcomes for children, schools, and their communities.*
>
> (AoEA website, 2024)

Index

Page numbers in *italics* denote figures.